NOTES ON BACH

NOTES ON BACH

20 Crucial Works

Conrad Wilson

William B. Eerdmans Publishing Company
Grand Rapids, Michigan

For Micaela, Cosima, Marcella, Rose, Eve, Charis, the two Bens
and all future Bachians.

© 2005 Conrad Wilson

First published 2005 by
SAINT ANDREW PRESS
Edinburgh

This edition published 2005
in the United States of America by
Wm. B. Eerdmans Publishing Company
255 Jefferson Ave. S.E., Grand Rapids, Michigan 49503

Printed in the United States of America

10 09 08 07 06 05   7 6 5 4 3 2 1

ISBN-10: 0-8028-2992-9
ISBN-13: 978-0-8028-2992-4

www.eerdmans.com

CONTENTS

FOREWORD

Why twenty? Obviously it is a device, one way of drawing attention to some of the masterpieces in a great composer's output. But at the same time it is a discipline and a challenge. Why choose these particular works and not others? The question and its answers are my reason for writing this book and its companions on other composers. In making my selection, I thought twenty works to be a good, sufficiently tight number. Increase it to thirty and choice becomes easier, perhaps too easy. Reduce it to ten and, in the case of great productive composers, you don't really have enough music wholly to justify what you are doing. Too many crucial works would have to be excluded, and the gaps would be glaring. So twenty it is, though not in the sense of a top twenty, because a crucial work does not actually have to be a great one, and the works are not listed – how could they be? – in any order of merit.

But each of them, it seems to me, needs to mark a special moment in its composer's life – perhaps a turning point, perhaps a sudden flash of inspiration, perhaps an intensifying of genius, as when Bach produced his *Actus Tragicus* at the age of 22, when Schubert produced his setting of Goethe's 'Gretchen am Spinnrade' at 17, or Mozart his G major Violin Concerto, K216, at 19, or Brahms his First Piano Concerto at 25.

Yet none of these composers was a prodigy as gifted as Mendelssohn, whose String Octet and whose *A Midsummer Night's Dream* overture were the most astounding teenage masterpieces of all time. But if there was nothing so arresting to be found among Mozart's or Schubert's numerous boyhood works, and certainly nothing among Brahms's, the change when it came was startling.

With Bach's first great cantata, Schubert's first great song, Mozart's first great concerto, Beethoven's and Mendelssohn's first great pieces of chamber music and Brahms's lengthy but inexorable perfecting of his First Piano Concerto came the shock of surprise in the form of an audacious new command of melody and accompaniment, a conspicuous leap in quality and, in the slow movement of the Mozart, a grasp of the mystery of beauty which made his two previous violin concertos, written in the same year, seem blandly impersonal exercises in composition.

Yet the third of Mozart's five violin concertos is not a masterpiece in the sense that *Don Giovanni* is, just as Schubert's boyhood String Quartet in E flat major, D87, for all its melodic beauty, is not as overwhelming as 'Death and the Maiden'. Nor, for that matter, does the fizz of Mendelssohn's early string symphonies have the passion of his A minor String Quartet, written very soon afterwards. Brahms's First Piano Concerto, on the other hand, is surely as great a work as he ever wrote.

It is not the aim of these books to set one masterpiece against another, or to suggest that early works are automatically less interesting than late ones. To regard a composer's output purely as a process of evolution is to fail inexcusably to accept a work on its own terms – a serious flaw in assessments of Schubert, who, according to many a pundit, did not 'find' himself until he was almost dead. In Mendelssohn, the division between what is 'early' and what is 'late' and what is the difference between them becomes less and less clearly demarcated.

So, early works are not being banned from these pages, even if it means the loss of some late ones. Nor is my decision to deal with the music chronologically based on any intrinsic belief that it reflects in some special way a composer's progress. The intention is simply to shed light on what was happening to him at the time he wrote a particular piece, where he was, what he was doing or experiencing, and how the music fits into the general pattern of his life and output. To go beyond this, by claiming that Haydn, for example, 'progressed' from his *Storm and Stress* symphonies to his *London* ones, or Mozart from his E flat major Piano Concerto, K271, to his E flat major, K482, is to undervalue his achievement as a whole.

So, no masterpiece has been omitted simply because its composer later in some way surpassed it. Some works are included simply because I adore them, or am prepared to defend them against the judgement of people who detest them. Liking a piece of music, we should always remember, is not the opposite of disliking it. It is a different condition altogether, and being able to explain why we like it is perhaps more important in the end than pronouncing on whether it is good music or bad.

Each of these twenty short essays is a species of what are traditionally known as programme notes – the descriptions to be found in printed concert or opera programmes of what is being performed that night. Donald Francis Tovey, one-time professor of music at Edinburgh University, was a famed and erudite pioneer of the form in the early twentieth century, and his collected *Essays in Musical Analysis* remain good to read, even if their style now seems old-fashioned and out of tune with today's musical thinking. Nor are they always accurate. Scholarship has progressed since Tovey's time.

Nevertheless, what Tovey wrote still towers over much of what passes for programme notes today. Even during my own post-Tovey boyhood, programme notes incorporated – as Tovey's did – musical examples because it was assumed that concert-goers could read music. Today, such notes would be branded elitist. To include musical terminology at all tends to be frowned upon. I have been asked why, in my own notes, I employ such terms as 'counterpoint', which nobody understands. But are football correspondents similarly chided for writing 'penalty' or 'free kick'? Somehow I think not. Though I am all against jargon, the use of an established, accessible musical term is preferable to a paragraph of explanation.

Concert programmes are now a dumbed-down art in which fatuous puffs about the performers occupy more space than the notes themselves, and adverts are given more space still. Traditional notes, as the chief executive of a concert organisation has remarked to me, are now 'irrelevant'. In the sense that most concerts today take place in darkened halls, he was perhaps right. But notes are written to be read before and after an event, as well as during it, and this book's intention is to fill that need.

In the sixteen years I spent editing the Edinburgh Festival's programme notes, there were a number of house rules which I worked out with the then Festival director, Peter Diamand, whose European outlook differed from, and was refreshingly less 'commercial' than, the British. Diamand's beliefs, which I shared, were that notes should contain facts rather than flimflam; that speculation was acceptable so long as it was informed; that notes should be coherently devised by a single writer for the contents of a single programme; that connections between one work and another should be mentioned; that the author, as Tovey once decreed, should act as counsel for the defence – Diamand detested notes which gave the impression that 'This is a bad work but let's perform it anyway'; and that artists' biographies should be confined to 150 words, should include no adjectives and should supply no information about what a performer would be performing in future seasons.

Though most of these principles have fallen by the wayside, they are still the ones to which I, as a note-writer, would prefer to adhere. In addition, I would say that, wherever possible, a work's place in musical history needs to be established; that its local connections (if any) should be mentioned; and that the writer has a responsibility to lure the reader into the music.

Some of the notes included in these pages are based on notes originally written for one musical organisation or another, but which have gone through a constant process of change, and which have now been changed yet again to suit the needs of a book about a single great composer. No note, whether for a concert programme or for something more permanent, should be merely 'drawn from stock'. Just as every performance of a work forms a part (however small) of that work's history, so every programme note should reflect the state – and status – of that work at the time the annotator is writing about it. Attitudes alter. Here, in this book, are twenty current attitudes (my own, but also quoting those of others) to twenty works that continue to matter.

Finally, a note on format. Each book begins with a fresh assessment of its subject composer and of the way he is performed at the start of the twenty-first century. Works are identified by opus or catalogue numbers, in Bach's case the Bach-Werke-Verzeichnis (BWV). Recordings are recommended at the end of each short essay. Books are listed for further reading, and technical terms are explained in a brief glossary.

CONRAD WILSON

Edinburgh, Scotland, and Introbio, Italy, 2005

INTRODUCTION

'Play Bach, Bach and more Bach.' The advice was Artur Rubinstein's, delivered to a novice pianist in a Hollywood film in which he himself flamboyantly performed Falla's *Ritual Fire Dance*, flinging his arms in the air in a very un-Bachian way. The time was the middle of the twentieth century, when the future of Bach's keyboard music – in performance terms at any rate – was anybody's guess. For pianists, piano teachers and those who liked big concert halls, the right instrument was bound to be the piano. For purists and those for whom Bach (1685–1750) represented something more intimate, then only the harpsichord could possibly produce the soft yet spiky, shimmering, gold-and-silver timbres so vital to Bach's music as the composer himself heard it. Pianists, in retaliation, pointed out that, by the end of his life, Bach knew about pianos, played them and would undoubtedly have proceeded to write for them. Indeed, for one of his last and greatest works, he did not specify any instrument at all. Harpsichordists remained unmoved by these assertions.

The authenticity movement, with its historically informed and increasingly adroit performances of all Bach's works, had not yet begun to burgeon. When it did so, and when it ceased to seem something small, over-specialised and often inept, it would alter the entire face of Bach performance. What was interesting, however, was that once it arrived, travelled the world and achieved widespread acceptance, it did not oust the piano. Today, some of the best performances of the *Goldberg Variations* – one of the most didactic but at the same time most adored of all Bach's works – are given on full-size concert grands.

Yet things, once they began to change, changed quickly, inspiring quantities of young ensembles to devote themselves almost exclusively to the music of Bach and his contemporaries. The Brandenburg concertos and orchestral suites no longer sounded slow, heavy and stolid. *The Art of Fugue*, severe though it seemed, successfully entered the public domain, so much so that it played a significant role in Vikram Seth's novel, *An Equal Music*. An entire millennial book was written around *The Musical Offering*, a similarly esoteric masterpiece – and by a former editor of *Time* magazine, of all unlikely people. The church cantatas, of which a mere 200 have survived out of a possible 300, were at last thoroughly explored and found to be crucial to his output.

The dark area of his organ music, which for most people lies outside the world of real Bach (though it was very real to him, especially in his younger days), began to find better instruments for its performance than the bulk of organs on which it was traditionally played. Though organ-fanciers are deemed to be a race apart, they are not all anoraks, as we tend to call such enthusiasts nowadays. When presented as an integer at the Edinburgh Festival by an exponent of the calibre of Peter Hurford, with the sun setting each evening behind the pipes of the fine modern organ in Greyfriars Kirk, this vast body of music proved to be not a daunting experience but an exhilarating, enthralling, sometimes even sensuous one. Such performances, however, remain rare.

The big choral works, once the domain of big Bach choirs, were scaled down to proportions which made sense of them, to the extent that very often today the four or five soloists are also the choristers. The instrumental music attracted performers – Rachel Podger, Andrew Manze, Reinhard Goebel, Pieter Wispelwey, Paulo Pandolfo – who understood its style, responded to its vitality and could strip inappropriate vibrato from string tone with the efficacy of a blowtorch.

These stylistic advances, each in itself only part of the picture and of no great consequence to the average concert-goer, together form a macrocosm which has helped to make Bach seem a composer even greater than before, more enthralling, more widely loved and performed – and for all the right reasons. Yet the music, as the scholar Joseph Kerman has put it, remains in some ways what it has always been – 'a limited, specialised, precious repertoire'. How it has broken its bounds, which in essence were the 125 miles of Germany from Eisenach to Dresden and the sixty from Cothen to Arnstadt, forms part of the mystery which is Bach.

Though his name today is synonymous with a bottled remedy for anxiety – invented by a Dr Bach – Bach's own two-part and three-part keyboard inventions, his four volumes of correctly (yet confusingly) entitled *Keyboard Exercises*, and above all the forty-eight preludes and fugues, can be said to have the same effect on those who hear them or are able to play them. The *Goldberg Variations*, indeed, were supposedly written to grip the attention of someone who suffered from the tedium of insomnia.

The word *Bach*, in German, means 'stream' – the slow movement of Beethoven's '*Pastoral*' symphony is named *An der Bach* ('Beside the Stream') – and music flowed from him throughout his career. Since he was not the sort of man to sit back and wait for inspiration to strike, his output was prodigious. The Bach dynasty, deeply musical, had already produced some fifty musicians before Johann Sebastian took his place among them, establishing his position at its heart and sustaining it by way of a number of by no means ungifted sons.

Although we no longer look on him as the fountainhead of all music – our enthusiasms today go back much further – that is not to say his stock has in any way depreciated. Indeed, it continues to rise. Never have we been more conscious of his achievement, or more able to recognise him for what he was: a great pivotal figure looking backwards through the history of German polyphony of which he formed the climax, and forwards to Liszt (whose variations on Bach's *Weinen, Klagen, Sorgen, Zagen* are so esteemed by Alfred Brendel), Busoni, Stravinsky and composers of more recent vintage. In England, even Elgar, devout Roman Catholic that he was, could not resist the allure of what Sir Thomas Beecham dismissed as Bach's 'Protestant counterpoint' and transcribed it for the size of orchestra that blares out the finale of the *Enigma Variations*.

Since 1850, when the Bach Gesellschaft was founded to publish his works, the range of his genius has been more and more widely recognised through the crystalline, exalted abstractions of *The Art of Fugue*, the keyboard pieces which were to inspire composers as different as Chopin and Shostakovich, and through the scale and intensity of the *Passion* settings in which, as Joseph Kerman has reminded us in his book *Opera as Drama*, Bach paved the way for Wagner's music dramas of more than a century later. Who would have thought, even thirty-or-so years ago, that the *Goldberg Variations*, with all their canons and other contrapuntal devices, would have become a household presence, recorded and rerecorded for a hungry public eager to treat them as background music of the choicest sort?

Tradition dictates that it is Mendelssohn whom we must thank above all for the widespread discovery or rediscovery of Bach, which began with his famous (abbreviated and altered) performance of the *St Matthew Passion* in Berlin in 1829. Yet there has been no period since Bach's death when musicians have been uninfluenced by the composer whose life, by modern standards, was so utterly private, so seemingly uninvolved with self-promotion other than within the tight-knit environment in which he worked.

We know of the profound impression he made on Mozart at Baron van Swieten's Sunday concerts of 'old' music. We know that Beethoven was reared on the forty-eight preludes and fugues, and by the age of 13 had been 'written up' by the Bonn press for his playing of them. We know that Schubert used them as teaching material, that Chopin composed his twenty-four preludes only after a deep study of them, and that he tuned his fingers before every recital by playing a Bach fugue (though he never did so in public). Mendelssohn's enthusiasm simply speeded the process of transforming Bach into public property; and when, years later, the Bach Gesellschaft neared the end of its mighty task, Brahms declared that this and the founding of the German Empire were the two major events of his life.

Once Stravinsky got his three great Russian ballets off his chest, Bach loomed increasingly over his output as he entered what became known as his neo-classical period, though neo-baroque or neo-Bachian would have been a better description of it. Yet was Bach not already to be detected somewhere amid the rhythmic racket of *The Rite of Spring*? Were the *Dumbarton Oaks* concerto, the Concerto in D for strings, the Concerto for piano and wind, the *Apollo* ballet music and the solo violin part in *The*

Soldier's Tale – in all of which Bach could easily be discerned – not various forms of purification of the earlier Stravinsky? Was the double fugue in the second movement of the *Symphony of Psalms* – one fugue played by the orchestra, the other sung by the chorus – not as profound a Bachian statement as any great composer had made in the twentieth century?

Bach's works have been hailed as a meditation on the nature of music itself. It is an apt description, succinctly explaining what the fugues in *The Art of Fugue* are about and also reminding us that the aims of all his instrumental pieces were originally largely private. Yet Bach himself never underestimated their value. When the forty-eight preludes and fugues were printed – simultaneously by three different publishers – half a century after his death, it was only the outcome of what he undoubtedly intended from the start.

One

1707
CANTATA NO. 106, *ACTUS TRAGICUS*,
BWV 106

Some people find it hard to believe that Bach was ever a boy. Not even the most assiduous of modern German Bachians, Christoph Wolff, could resist adding the subtitle *The Learned Musician* to his millennial biography, or proclaiming him to be above all an 'academic' and a 'scholar'. But, although the traditional notion of a Bach old before his time still runs deep, he was in many ways a young man like any other, a maverick and a musical firebrand more dangerous than most of his contemporaries.

Though facts about his early years remain in short supply, which is why we cling so tightly to what we know about his maturity, we are at least aware of his pilgrimage – from one side of Germany to another, on foot at the age of 20 – to see and hear Dietrich Buxtehude play the organ in Lübeck. We also know that, in the same year, he stood accused in Arnstadt of drawing his sword against a student and calling him a *Zippelfaggotist*, a vulgar term for an incompetent bassoonist.

In personality, he was notoriously insubordinate, storming out of meetings and enraging his superiors by extending his holidays without permission (on one occasion by three months), failing to show loyalty to those who employed him (once so blatantly that he was thrown into prison), and complaining constantly about poor pay and working conditions. Not even the audacious young Mozart in Salzburg could be said to have got himself more frequently into hot water or to have put his job more seriously at risk.

Some of Bach's self-confident aggressiveness, no doubt, can be traced back to the fact that by the age of 10 he was an orphan. The world, he became convinced, was out to get him, and he took steps to prevent this happening. Yet it was not just his parents who so rapidly died. From childhood onwards, he was surrounded by the deaths of relatives, colleagues and, at the age of 35, his first wife (returning from a trip, he found her not only dead but already buried).

The Bachs were nevertheless a vast and complex family, living up to their name (German for 'stream') and spreading themselves all over Germany. One of Bach's earliest harpsichord works, of no great importance yet well worth listening to, was his picturesque *Capriccio on the Departure of a Beloved Brother*, with movements graphically entitled 'Friends gather and try to dissuade him from departing', 'They picture the dangers which may befall him', 'The friends lament', 'Since he cannot be dissuaded, they say farewell', 'Aria of the postilion' and 'Fugue in imitation of the postilion's horn'.

Likewise, his Cantata No. 106, known as the *Actus Tragicus*, is a notably explicit product of his early years, its title so arresting yet so curiously un-Bachian in its theatricality that you could almost think it to have been supplied by someone else. The eloquence of this funeral cantata, however, is as potent as its name. All we know about it is that it was composed at the age of 22 in tribute to – whom? Posterity claims it was either Bach's Uncle Tobias, who died in the summer of 1707, or else the sister of a friend, who died leaving a husband and four children, just as Bach's mother had done fourteen years before.

For all the starkness of its title, however, the work begins gently, to the strains of a pair of two sweetly warbling recorders, a pair of darker-toned violas da gamba, and an organ. Yet this short introduction, as John Eliot Gardiner has claimed in an essay on the music, is twenty of the most heart-rending bars in all Bach. The melodic interweaving of the instruments disconcertingly slides in and out of phase. Later, in the central arioso movement, the solo soprano's poignant plea, 'Yes, come, Lord Jesus', is voiced more than fifteen times. In its evocation of death, the music descends through a series of minor keys until it trickles to a stop at the mathematically precise centre of the work, which Bach marks with a pause sign.

Then, mostly in the major, it starts to rise again until it reaches the key of E flat – Mozart's future Masonic key – in which it had begun. The message evoked by the music is clear. As Gardiner points out, the descent has told us that 'in the midst of life we are in death', the ascent that 'in the midst of death we are in life'. The result, he says, comes as close as any piece of music he knows towards piercing the membrane that separates the material world from whatever lies beyond. Bach's musical argument is movingly and deftly clinched, his mathematical awareness both sublime and in its prime.

Public awareness of the work's greatness, however, has only now begun to grow, thanks to the handful of conductors who have chosen to champion it. Yet, under its formal title of Cantata No. 106, this forerunner of the great flow of works produced years later for St Thomas's, Leipzig, remains a rarity, containing nothing as famously melodious as 'Jesu Joy of Man's Desiring' (Cantata No. 147) or 'Sheep May Safely Graze' (Cantata No. 208).

Its funereal connotations have been, no doubt, a deterrent factor. But death, and the anticipation of death, loomed large in Bach's vocal music. His family life was a long history of bereavement. His cantatas, as researchers have remarked, were sometimes performed around the bed of the deceased (thereby exposing the choirboys, as one health-conscious authority has pointed out, to a dangerously germ-laden environment).

Today, a good performance of a work such as his Cantata No. 82 ('Ich habe genug'), in which physical life on earth is portrayed as a miserable prelude to the rewards which await the Christian in heaven, will reduce an audience to silence or even to tears. It is not surprising that singers as expressive as Hans Hotter and Dietrich Fischer-Dieskau became so closely identified with it, though rather more startling that the eloquent Lorraine Hunt Lieberson went so far as to take part in Peter Sellers's dramatisation of it (along with the Cantata No. 199, 'My Heart Swims in Blood'), in which the singer portrayed someone dying of cancer in hospital.

At least two recordings of the *Actus Tragicus* possess the same searing yet consoling effect as Lieberson's of these two other death-conscious works. Sir John Eliot Gardiner's, with the Monteverdi Choir and English Baroque Soloists, formed part of a pilgrimage which he undertook on the 250th anniversary of Bach's death to perform and record all the surviving church cantatas in different churches around the world. The intent, beautifully blended account of it, with Nancy Argenta as soprano soloist, was recorded in London at St John's, Smith Square, with the Mourning Ode, BWV 198, and the motet *O Jesu Christ, mein's Lebens Licht* as appendages (Archiv 463 581-2).

No less intimately voiced is the performance by Konrad Junghanel and the Cantus Cölln, with three other cantatas, one of them the magnificent *Weinen, Klagen, Sorgen, Zagen* ('Weeping, Lamenting, Worrying, Fearing') (BWV 12), forming the remainder of a generous disc (Harmonia Mundi

HMC 801694). Lorraine Hunt Lieberson's overwhelming account of Cantatas Nos 82 and 199 is accompanied, more expressively than stylishly, by the Orchestra of Emmanuel Music conducted by Craig Smith (Nonesuch 7559-79692-2).

Two

1708–17
TOCCATA, ADAGIO AND FUGUE IN C MAJOR, BWV 564

Just as Bach arranged other people's music, so Ferruccio Busoni (1866–1924) arranged Bach's. Tradition has it that Busonified Bach is Bach played big and, depending on your attitude, Bach played improperly. But, though his famous piano transcription of the D minor Chaconne for solo violin is certainly bigger, in sheer weight of tone, than the original, his various piano transcriptions of Bach's organ music inevitably sound smaller than a performance of one of these works on some grand cathedral organ.

Sheer weight of tone, in any case, is never wholly the point of the metamorphoses Bach went through at Busoni's hands. As one of the most formidable pianists of his period, and as one of the mightiest musical intellects, Busoni was bound to do more to Bach than merely inflate him. What he did, whether soft or loud, reflective or audacious, has often been dismissed as kitsch; but that is hardly the right word for the process of contemplation, speculation and experimentation through which Busoni put Bach's music so as to produce what we have come to call Bach–Busoni. But, if Busoni's message is to reach us successfully, it must come from a pianist similarly contemplative, speculative and experimental, who can read Busoni's mind as well as Bach's, and recognise that – as Busoni himself put it – the performance of any work is in itself a form of transcription.

Dating from 1900, the Busoni version of the C major Toccata, Adagio and Fugue bears out his belief that Bach's organ music, performed on a piano, should not sound like a piano imitating an organ. Preferring, he said, to conceive it for an 'imaginary' instrument, he managed to make the three movements – the fits-and-starts energy of the toccata, the stealthy, almost static *adagio*, the jaunty fugue – sound from time to time curiously like a Vivaldi concerto, reminding us (though obviously unintentionally) that Bach himself was an expert transcriber of his Italian contemporary.

In Italy, children are traditionally told by their parents 'non toccare', meaning 'not to touch'. But toccatas, both before and after Bach's time, were 'touch' pieces, through which a keyboard player could try out a new instrument, whether organ or harpsichord, or simply flex his fingers, displaying his brilliance or delicacy of touch in the process. For Bach, particularly in his younger days, the testing of instruments formed part of his work, and he was famously expert at it. Usually, and for obvious reasons, the test pieces he composed or improvised would be demonstrative, focusing on evenness of part-writing and incorporating rapid flurries of notes from top to bottom of the register, but it could also be slow and expressive, all within the confines of a single work.

But the big C major Toccata, with its multiplicity of short phrases, its flourishes, rests, echo effects, deliberate hesitations and tendency to tease, is something more than just a touch piece. The minor-key slow movement, its poignant melodic line underpinned by soft, spaced-out chords (and a sudden, climactically loud, slashing one) could almost come from Vivaldi's *Four Seasons*. As for the final fugue, it is a study in imperturbable Bachian poise and flow, splendidly sustained in Busoni's makeover.

For all its grandeur, however, this work remains surprisingly under-recorded. Scan the record guides and you will have trouble tracking it down. But Kun-Woo Paik, at least, gives it pride of place in a bundle of transcriptions which convey a sonorous idea of Busoni's by no means despicable achievement (Decca 467 358-2).

For the young Bach, the period up to 1717 was a time of toccatas. In 1705, at the age of 20, he had taken his famous cross-country walk all the way from Arnstadt in eastern Germany to Lübeck on the Danish border to meet Dietrich Buxtehude and be inspired by the great organist's extravagant 'stylus fantasticus'. Less inspirational, it seemed, was the offer of Buxtehude's daughter's hand in marriage, which Handel had already significantly declined. Nevertheless, Bach stayed longer in Lübeck than he originally intended, and the series of seven substantial keyboard toccatas he composed during the succeeding decade were major products of Buxtehude's influence on him.

Bach's most famous toccata is the one for organ in D minor – though modern authorities have begun to claim, very convincingly, that it was originally for solo violin – which serves as prelude to the equally famous fugue in the same key. But, being very short, it is not wholly typical of his structurally elaborate keyboard toccatas, to which fugues are not attachments but an intrinsic part of the toccata's design.

This increased cogency is very much what occurs in the magnificent C minor Toccata, a benchmark work in the form, whose spiky opening flourish leads into a broodingly expressive and 'affecting' adagio, and from there to a powerfully propelled fugue. After a reflective back-reference to the adagio, the fugue resumes, speeding now inexorably towards its resolution. The result, then, is a coherent unity rather than two pieces grafted together and connected only by the key in which they are written. True, the great harpsichordist Wanda Landowska claimed not to find them coherent at all; but that was perhaps because their rhetoric, for her, obscured their logic. Heard as big baroque soliloquies, however, they make strong, enthralling sense. Nor do they lack variety of utterance, as the works in sombre G minor and radiant D major amply demonstrate.

Though clearly intended for the harpsichord, this is music which transfers without difficulty to the modern concert grand. Among today's exponents of it, the Canadian pianist Angela Hewitt is justly celebrated. Indeed, her CD of these toccatas, impeccably recorded by Hyperion (CDA 67310), is one of the very best of her Bach surveys. If, on the other hand, you can tolerate the poorer sound quality, Hewitt's sensationally unpredictable but thoroughly inspired Canadian predecessor, Glenn Gould, delivers the music with even fuller command of its theatricality (Sony SMK 87762-3).

Three

(Allegro moderato)   Allegro

Bach's life, it is often said, was notoriously, frustratingly uneventful, particularly for biographers and writers of programme notes. There are a handful of famous stories, constantly quoted. There are official documents, dry but useful. There is the big obituary — big but not big enough — written by the sharpest of his sons, Carl Philipp Emanuel, in tandem with a former student, Johann Agricola, four years after his death. For the inquiring Bach biographer, it is not a lot.

The tale of the Brandenburg Concertos, at least, is fully authenticated. Or is it? In its standard version, it runs as follows. During the six years, from 1717 to 1723, which Bach spent at the court of Prince Leopold of Anhalt-Cothen, he visited Berlin to buy a new clavier for his master. While there, he played before Christoph Ludwig, Margrave of Brandenburg, who asked if he could see some samples of Bach's work. That, at any rate, is theoretically why Bach sent him the six concertos which have come to be known as the Brandenburgs.

'I have taken the liberty', wrote the composer on the autograph score, 'of fulfilling my very humble duty to Your Royal Highness with these Concerti which I have scored for several instruments.' The date on the title page is 1721, conclusive proof, or so you would think, that that was when they were composed. But not necessarily so. Christoph Wolff, latest of Bach's scholarly biographers, plausibly claims that, despite the written date, they were composed not during Bach's spell in Cothen at all but some years earlier in Weimar, where he was court organist and chamber musician. Certainly, there is no evidence that the Margrave of Brandenburg ever performed, let alone paid for, the six works, which Bach himself subsequently pillaged – a revised version of the first movement of No. 3, incorporating oboes and horns, forms part of the Cantata No. 174.

Then there is the question of the music itself. How fast should it be played? How slow? Sir Adrian Boult's stately performances of these concertos spoke of a Bach very different from Trevor Pinnock's several decades later. Karl Münchinger's versions, for all their progressiveness, were soon outstripped by Nikolaus Harnoncourt's. Harnoncourt himself now seems no match for Giovanni Antonini, whose ensemble named Il Giardino Armonico ('The Harmonic Garden') moves so fast that it is in danger of driving right past the music. Whether Bach needs a conductor at all has long been a moot point, demonstrating the adage – with Herbert von Karajan's symphony-orchestra-plus-two-harpsichords-with-Karajan-himself-on-one-of-them treatment of Bach as a case in point – that the greater the conductor the worse the performance.

Quite apart from questions of tempo, style, weight, authenticity and attitude, however, each concerto presents performers with specific problems of its own. In the case of the Third Concerto, what is to be done about the gap in the middle, where two chords are all that remain of what is presumably but not necessarily a vanished slow movement? Some conductors make do with tweaking and extending these chords. Some add a substitute movement from another of Bach's works. The two extant movements, a sturdy opening *allegro* and a swinging, swirling gigue, are designed to be played by three even groups of strings – violins, violas and cellos, nine players in all, or what could be called a sort of triple trio, plus harpsichord continuo – with every line of the music a solo line, and each instrument playing its role in a finely detailed contrapuntal whole.

Of the six concertos, the Third is inevitably the most succinct and traditionally the most popular, not least because big or biggish orchestras as well as chamber ensembles can perform it – or think they can. Its robust rhythms keep the music spinning, no matter how many, or how few, players are involved. For an audience, it is the ideal springboard into the other five works.

Whether the Brandenburgs should be regarded as an entity is another matter, however. Though Bach saw the point of marketing them as concertos 'for several instruments', their tonal variety – ranging from the horns, oboes, violino piccolo (a high-pitched baroque violin) and bassoon of the First Concerto to the buoyant concerted violas and lower-toned strings of the Sixth – is seldom shown to advantage within the framework of a single and inevitably overlong concert. They are works to be savoured one or two at a time, not gorged upon.

Yet, as a baroque portfolio they undeniably form a unity which requires you to be aware that each concerto has its context and, within that context, some special state-of-the-art feature of its own. In the Third Concerto, this derives from the compressed energy and balance of a tight-knit group of strings. In the First, the clash between the horns and other instruments provides the piquancy, along with a grand minuet finale spun out by three pungent interludes. In the Second, a mercurial high trumpet rides the texture. In the Fourth, warbling flutes or recorders intermingle sweetly – and ultimately in a spirited jam session – with a solo violin.

The Fifth is a keyboard concerto in which the harpsichord gradually emerges from its background role and becomes a fully fledged solo voice – so much so that in the first movement it breaks free from the rest of the orchestra in an extended and exhilarating cadenza. Though nothing quite like this had ever been written before, Bach had other surprises up his sleeve. The slow movement, a trio in which the violin, flute and harpsichord have the platform to themselves and the orchestra is again shaken off, is no mere sonata movement transferred to a concerto but a miracle of ever-changing interplay. As for the finale, it is a captivating eye and ear illusion whereby the written rhythms sound utterly different from how they look on paper.

To buy a recording of one of the Brandenburg concertos today usually entails buying all six. But this is no hardship, considering their level of inspiration and the quantity of fine performances there now are. For sheer zip, Giovanni Antonini's Giardino Armonico would take some beating (Warner Elatus 2564 60658-2 and 60803-2). These are baroque performances of the lightest, most captivating sort. Not even Nikolaus Harnoncourt and his Vienna Concentus Musicus outclass them in two historic recordings of these works (go for the second on Teldec Ultima 0630-18944-2).

At the other extreme, there is Wilhelm Furtwängler, who shows what a great conductor can do to the Fifth Concerto when he not only conducts the Vienna Philharmonic but also himself plays the harpsichord part on a piano. This is Bach in terms of late Beethoven, with the first-movement cadenza transformed – in one commentator's memorable phrase – into a transcendental sermon. The recording forms part of an eight-disc Furtwängler retrospective which includes, for good measure, Beethoven's Ninth Symphony and other performances dating from the last years of the controversial conductor's life (Orfeo C409 048L).

Four

1717-22
ITALIAN CONCERTO IN F MAJOR, BWV 971

(Allegro)   Andante   Presto

Handel, born in the Saxon city of Halle, worked productively in Italy before settling in London. Mozart, born in Salzburg, travelled widely in Europe before settling in Vienna. Haydn, in his later years, made long and lauded journeys to London and Paris. Vivaldi, born in Venice, died in Vienna. Domenico Scarlatti, born in Naples, died in Madrid. But Bach, 'parsimonious and prudent', did not travel at all – or so it is traditionally said.

In fact, Bach travelled quite a lot, from town to town, court to court, church to church, organ to organ, harpsichord to harpsichord, but never outside Germany. His long trek to Lübeck to learn from Buxtehude, however, was no mere bagatelle in his life. Brief though his visit was, its influence on him was profound. Nor was his famous trip to Berlin, forever afterwards associated with the Brandenburg concertos, merely the equivalent of a weekend break. Potsdam, too, went down in Bach history, not just because he journeyed there to see Carl Philipp Emanuel, the most musically progressive of his sons, who had been appointed harpsichordist to Frederick the Great, but also because his arrival at Sans-Souci, Frederick's residence, prompted the flautist king to exclaim to his court: 'Ladies and gentlemen, Old Bach is here'. Whether his remark was what we would now call offensively ageist, whether it was merely meant to differentiate between father and son, or whether it was ever made at all, we do not know for sure. What we do know is that Bach's age at the time was 62.

Far from being a provincial dry-as-dust scholar, then, Bach was a sophisticated musician, an expert on keyboards who kept his eyes and ears open and whose advice was constantly in demand. Moreover, he knew very well what was happening musically in France and Italy, found new inspiration in it, and composed with genius in the French and Italian styles while retaining his own German contrapuntal skills and self-discipline. If he never strayed too far from home – though he had no long-term home until he moved to Leipzig at the age of 38 – it was because he did not need to. But the influence of France is to be found in his numerous dance suites, and of Italy in his adoption, via Vivaldi, of the three-movement Italian concerto format.

The point about Bach's Italian Concerto, however, is that it is not really a concerto at all – at least in the conventional sense whereby a soloist interacts with a body of instrumentalists. On the contrary, the music represents Bach's response to the Italian concerto style in a work where soloist and orchestra turn out to be one and the same person. Though the contrasts built into the music make this perfectly clear, Bach underlined them by marking the solos *piano* (meaning quiet) and the orchestral passages *forte* (implying louder). Such specifications may today seem less than revolutionary, but in Bach's time they had real novelty value – not until he was 50 did he give performers such specifically eye-catching guidelines.

Even the overall title which Bach originally bestowed on this work and on its companion piece, the French Ouverture in B minor, was not exactly eye-catching. Together they formed his *Clavierübung II* ('Keyboard Practice volume two'), which seems a grey and abstract way in which to refer to a work as racy and colourful as the Italian Concerto. But, as one Bach authority has pointed out, *Clavierübung II* probably did not signify 'music to practise on a keyboard'. In Bach's day, there was no such thing as keyboard practice of the sort which Mozart knew about, whereby music teachers taught their pupils technique. What Bach seems more likely to have meant was music in which the Italian and French styles were put into practice for the benefit of performers. In that case, the title *Clavierübung II*, for all its dryness, would be perfectly appropriate.

It does not, however, draw attention to the sheer virtuosity of the Italian Concerto, which is one of its special features. Not only does the performer have two important roles to play, he has to be a master of the art of contrast, distinguishing between the sound of a solo instrument and of an orchestra with the help, in Bach's day, of a two-manual harpsichord. At the same time, the music has a rigorous symmetry which makes no allowances for flamboyance, though it certainly permits expressiveness.

In this respect, though it was not published until the 1730s, the Italian Concerto is typical of the works which Bach produced during his period as Kapellmeister to Prince Leopold of Anhalt-Cothen, a sternly Calvinist dynasty which frowned on the singing of religious music in chapel but encouraged Bach to find other outlets for his inspiration. Though deprived of composing cantatas and chorales, he discovered Prince Leopold to be an otherwise congenial employer who was not only a talented amateur musician but a deep admirer of Bach's music. Despite the austerity of its religion, Cothen's atmosphere turned out to be otherwise musically relaxed; and Bach, still a vigorous young man in his thirties, felt able to experiment as much as he liked in composing for the court musicians.

From this period date some of Bach's finest instrumental masterpieces: the violin and keyboard concertos, the orchestral suites, the first book of the forty-eight preludes and fugues, the partitas and sonatas for solo violin, the six cello suites, the French and English harpsichord suites and harpsichord partitas. And, of course, the Italian Concerto. With its striking juxtapositions of thick, fully coupled two-manual registration and the gentler timbres of the solo stop and single manual, this is harpsichord music at its most brilliant. Yet, as a feat of keyboard legerdemain, it has appealed to pianists just as much as to harpsichordists – though only the latter instrument can realise its shimmering, terraced sonorities in the way Bach intended.

Authenticity, however, is not always the answer. The wrong harp-sichordist playing the wrong harpsichord in the wrong hall is not preferable to the right pianist and the right piano in the right surroundings. On disc, the French harpsichordist Christophe Rousset gets to the heart of the matter with a performance in which authenticity and aplomb are perfectly combined. The concerto itself is here combined with the French Ouverture in B minor and the great Chromatic Fantasy and Fugue in D minor to form the most riveting of harpsichord recitals (Decca Universal Classics 4761704).

Such performances, however, demand to be heard in a small baroque hall or else through headphones. To remain part of what Alfred Brendel describes as the 'living concert repertoire', the music requires something different, and it is Brendel himself who supplies it on the rare occasions he plays Bach on the piano in a big modern auditorium. His recording of the Italian Concerto does not sound like a transcription of harpsichord music any more than it sounds like anything but itself. The instrument, in a sense, is irrelevant. It is Bach who matters, and the piano is simply the instrument (or, as Stravinsky would have said, the conduit) through which the lines and rhythms and counterpoints flow. In this respect, the playing, as also in the Chromatic Fantasy and Fugue and in the handful of preludes which complete the disc, is a revelation (Philips 442 400-2).

Five

1720
PARTITA NO. 3 IN E MAJOR FOR SOLO VIOLIN, BWV 1006

Preludio	Loure	Gavotte en Rondeau
Menuett 1 and 2	Bourrée	Gigue

Bach composed six masterpieces for what he described as 'Violino senza Basso accompagnato', or what in English translation was long known as 'unaccompanied' violin. Perfectly explicit though it was, the term carried misleading overtones in that it seemed to imply the absence of some established ingredient, such as the presence of another instrument to fill in the harmony.

As a result, the 'Sei solo' (six solos), as Bach very simply (and imprecisely) called them, were thought to be in some way incomplete, and therefore unsatisfactory, as well as extraordinarily difficult to perform. Indeed, during the century after Bach's death, other composers sometimes took it upon themselves to supply the 'missing' accompaniments – an act which, however well intended, was irrelevant, since the whole point of these works, and the whole nature of their mastery, was that the violinist was his own accompanist.

Yet the effect of the music was neither freakish nor cerebral. In his partitas and sonatas for solo violin, and in his parallel series of suites for solo cello, Bach demonstrated that he could handle harmony, modulation and melody on a single instrument with such expressiveness that the outcome was some of the most sensuous music ever composed. By such devices as double-stopping, he made contrapuntal voices sing out of the music with astounding definition. If this was technical wizardry, it was wizardry of the highest order, veering between the sublime austerity of the three solo sonatas and the sweetness of the more relaxed partitas, or suites, with which Bach chose to alternate them.

In this respect, the sublime good cheer of the E major Partita's mercurial opening prelude – one of the great examples of the art of perpetual motion – has won widespread fame outside the context of the work's five other movements. Only the high seriousness of the D minor Partita's great and very different concluding chaconne similarly makes its point without the support of the rest of the work. Yet both these partitas underline Bach's interest in dance rhythms, whether in the simple structures of the E major Partita's loure (named after a rustic French bagpipe), gavotte, minuet, bourrée and gigue, or in the allemande, courante, sarabande and gigue which pave the way for the much more complex unfurling of the slow triple-time chaconne in the D minor work, in effect a huge, slow, stately dance based with grand severity on an obsessively recurring jerky rhythm.

Each of these six works, which together form what we like to think of as the fountainhead of the solo violin repertoire (though they were not in fact the first of their kind), is extraordinary in its technical and emotional range. Each gains its dramatic colouring from Bach's choice of major or minor key. Each, if it does not seem too fanciful to say so, can be compared with a monologue delivered by a great actor, the differences between one performance and another being as arresting as those between a Gielgud and an Olivier declaiming Shakespeare.

The prelude and fugue which open the C major Sonata are grand and severe, the swaying introductory *adagio* so slow that its dissonances are massive and sustained in their effect, the fugue inexorable in its steady, almost mechanised progress, the juxtaposition of the two movements conveying a continual, deliberate sense of strain which the music needs to suggest if it is to make its impact. These works, no matter how fearlessly they can nowadays be performed, should never sound easy.

The *andante* of the A minor Sonata is another marvellous movement, warm, quietly rocking, seemingly endless in the way it slowly unrolls, yet actually quite short. But the greatest movement of all, the summit of these 'solos' and the obverse of the prelude to the E major Sonata, is the chaconne from the D minor Partita. How these two big works differ from each other is very interesting. In the E major Partita, the emphasis is on light, amiable, major-key dances. The loure in three-four time is typically gentle, lilting, slightly wistful, though rich triple-stopping gives it a degree of grandeur. The gavotte in rondo form, like the prelude, stands easily on its own, and its catchy, much-repeated tune helps it to do so. The two minuets are more relaxed, the bourrée makes use of echo effects, and the cartwheeling gigue sustains the lightness of touch.

But the D minor chaconne is another matter. Tacked on, or so it might seem, at the end of a spinning, athletic gigue – the expected finale of a Bach suite – it could at first be assumed to be some sort of afterthought. In fact, it is the work's mighty destination, music of awe-inspiring resourcefulness, moving slowly and relentlessly through sequences of variations, increasing and diminishing in intensity and elaboration, and testing the performer's technique to the utmost.

Yet baroque austerity, on which the whole concept of such music is founded, does not exclude beauty of tone. There is one moment of special magic, adored by all Bach-lovers, when with a sudden hush the key changes from stern D minor to the glow of D major, revealing Bach to have been unmistakably a romantic composer at heart. This passage forms not only the middle section but also the emotional core of the whole movement. Like the cello suite in the same key, the music also possesses more than a hint of sorrow, wholly in keeping with the fact that Bach composed it, or so people like to think, in memory of his first wife,

Maria Barbara, who died in 1720 at the age of 35 while Bach was visiting Carlsbad, a popular spa. When he set off, she was in good health. When he returned, she was in her grave.

A protean piece, the D minor chaconne exists in a variety of arrangements, most of them monstrous, some of them inspired. Busoni's, for piano, remains the most famous, turning it into an uninhibited exploration of the resonance of a concert grand. Its justification, if it needs one, lies in Bach's own deep belief in the art of transcription, his unrivalled ability to change violin music into keyboard music, or vice versa, in such a way that nobody could guess which was the original.

Though Busoni's piano version of the chaconne states grandly and in expanded harmonies what the original violin version says more subtly, its effect in the hands of a pianist with an ear for baroque sonority is undeniably impressive. To deem it 'inferior' to Bach's austere original would be to approach it through ears rigidly attuned to authenticity. Busoni's listeners would not have heard it that way, nor would Brahms's – though Brahms, it must be said, brought his own strictness to his piano transcription of the chaconne by writing it for left hand alone, in keyboard terms a stupendous feat. In the end, perhaps, we should remember that Bach himself saw nothing bizarre in reworking the prelude to his E major Partita for solo violin in an orchestral version incorporating trumpets, drums and organ.

Among recordings of Bach's solo violin sonatas and partitas, Arthur Grumiaux's has long stood out for its authority and keen intensity of articulation (Philips 464 673-2). But Rachel Podger, playing on a baroque violin, is perhaps even more remarkable and certainly no less accurate, above all in the circling vitality of the C major Sonata's final *allegro assai* (Channel Classics CCSSEL 2498).

Six

1720
SUITE No. 6 IN D MAJOR FOR SOLO CELLO, BWV 1012

Prelude   Allemande   Courante

Sarabande   Gavotte 1 and 2   Gigue

Brahms and his contemporaries enjoyed tampering with Bach's works for solo cello and solo violin, transcribing them for other instruments, rendering them more (or sometimes less) playable, and adding the keyboard parts they thought Bach had omitted from the originals. Brahms, at least, treated these matters with genuine seriousness. When he played his own testingly left-handed piano version of the great violin chaconne from the D minor Partita, he said it made him 'feel like a violinist'.

Yet, in many respects these nineteenth-century adaptations missed, or ignored, the point of the cello suites in the same way as that of the violin sonatas and partitas. Bach's cello suites were written for what the composer described as 'Violoncello solo senza Basso', or what in English translation became known as 'unaccompanied' cello. Perfectly explicit though it was, the term carried misleading overtones in that it seemed to imply the omission of some established ingredient, such as the use of a harpsichord to complete the harmony.

As a result, the music was often felt to be in some way unsatisfactory (as well as awkward) to perform. But, however well intended, the act of supplying the 'missing' accompaniments was irrelevant. The whole reason for the writing of these works, and the whole nature of their mastery, lay in the fact that the cellist was his or her own accompanist.

Yet the effect, as already pointed out, was neither freakish nor cerebral. In his six suites for solo cello, which form a sequel to the series of partitas and sonatas for solo violin, Bach demonstrated that he could handle harmony, modulation and melody on a single instrument with such expressiveness that the result was some of the richest, most sensuous music ever composed.

By such devices as double- or triple-stopping – which meant playing on two or three strings simultaneously – he made contrapuntal voices ring out with astounding definition, veering in the final D major suite between the sublime abstract austerity of the prelude and allemande, the fleetness of the courante and gigue, the rich, slow sonorities of the sarabande, and the sweetly melodious gracefulness of the gavottes.

Not all of Bach's cello suites were actually written for the cello as we know it, and this was one which was not. By calling the fifth of the six works a 'suite discordable', because he wanted the A string of the instrument to be tuned down to G, he had provided himself with fresh harmonic and tonal potential. In the sixth suite, he went further, drawing upon the resources of a small five-stringed cello, or *violoncello piccolo*, whose range was substantially higher than that of a standard cello.

Yet it was not to produce five-note chords that Bach did this. His aim was to write high singing melodies for an essentially deep-toned instrument, without putting the music out of the reach of an ordinary four-stringed cello. The result, as every cellist knows, is more challenging to play, and often places intonation under stress, but the work's effects are not impossible to achieve; indeed, the audible sense of strain adds a further factor to the intensity of the music.

The way the prelude screws itself up into the cello stratosphere illustrates the element of struggle which is, or should be, a vital feature of all these solo works, making them the special experiences they are. But why did Bach write them? What are they about? Do they have a deliberate running order? Certainly they grow progressively longer, the sixth (running to half an hour) being by far the biggest – though that does not necessarily mean it was the last to be written, or was intended to form the climax of the series.

Not much is known about the provenance of these pieces, other than that they date from Bach's six-year stint as Kapellmeister at Cothen. Nobody knows who originally played them (Carl Friedrich Abel, the family friend whose name is often associated with them, was not born until 1723) or whether they were presented singly, or in pairs, or in some other manner. What seems certain is that they were not performed all at once, in a single marathon recital, as some modern cellists – Yo-Yo Ma, Pieter Wispelwey – are prone to do. To Bach, though not to everybody today, this would surely have seemed absurd.

In a way, however, they form a very private small gallery of musical self-portraits. Pablo Casals, the first great public exponent of these works, hailed them (in numerical order) as 'optimistic', 'tragic', 'heroic', 'grandiose', 'tempestuous' and 'bucolic'. Other performers hear them differently, though the second suite, which is in D minor, does seem to possess some of the tragic dimension of the violin partita in the same key, with its great closing chaconne.

Yet, to claim that these suites are not 'about' anything at all, that they are neither sad nor happy, and that all the performer (and listener) can do is simply to absorb them, is a description of them as valid as any other. To note that some movements reach their point of highest tension halfway through, and that others achieve this just before their end, may seem a dry way to approach music as 'expressive' – i.e. evocative, emotive? – as this. But the marvellous thing is that the chords and absence of chords, the contrasts between lyricism and drama, the melodies which are 'accompanied' and those which are not, the short phrases and long phrases, and the sheer versatility of the music are what help to make these suites what they are.

The cellists who, for posterity, have recorded their performances of these works include Casals himself, though some would argue today that his playing sounds so assertive that it gets in the way of the music. As one commentator has put it, his bow slices through Bach's chords like a meat-cleaver. Pierre Fournier, in his famous recording from the early 1960s, comes closer to the truth – even, some would say, the soul – of the six works in a performance where classical rigour and romantic poetry combine to unerring effect (DG 449 711-2GOR2).

In matters of intimacy, fantasy and lightness of touch, however, he is surely surpassed by the Dutch cellist, Pieter Wispelwey, one of a new generation of style-conscious interpreters who find their own way to the heart of the matter. His use of a five-stringed violoncello piccolo in the final suite adds not only authenticity but also exceptional eloquence to his playing (Channel Classics CCS 12298).

Perhaps even more fascinating – and certainly in a class of its own – is Paulo Pandolfo's recording in which he adapts all six suites to his own instrument, the viola da gamba, on which he is a world expert. Far from sounding pedagogic, his playing resounds with radiant life. The instrument, which looks like a cello without a spike, sheds its own warm light on the music without distorting it, particularly when played with such accuracy and sensitivity. The box in which the two discs are packaged, with an imaginatively theatrical note by the performer, is itself a work of art (Glossa Platinum GCD 920405).

Seven

1720
ENGLISH SUITE NO. 6 IN D MINOR, BWV 811

Prelude	Allemande	Courante	Sarabande
Double		Gavotte 1 and 2	Gigue

Why some of Bach's keyboard suites are called 'English' and others 'French' is a question to which nobody – including Bach himself – has supplied a satisfactory answer. But, until it can be proved that the titles were Bach's own, there seems little point in looking for English features in the English suites which will differentiate them in some recognisable way from the Frenchness of the French ones. The music appears to possess no peculiarly English theme, no specific English accent, quirk, colouring or melodic reference. The style, indeed, seems just as French as that of the French suites, at least in the sense that most of the movements are characteristic French dances – sarabande, gavotte, gigue – of the sort employed by baroque composers (of whatever nationality) when they wrote suites of instrumental or orchestral pieces.

So the claim made by Johann Forkel, Bach's first biographer, that the six English suites were composed for 'an Englishman of rank' can be immediately discarded. For a start, Bach did not compose these works as a set, though he ultimately saw the wisdom of thus collecting them into one volume – he was nothing if not a practical composer. More significant, perhaps, was their alternative title of 'Great' suites, since it was in size, rather than Englishness, that they differed from the six smaller, simpler, less abstract, more immediately melodious French suites, which he wrote as teaching pieces for his second wife, Anna Magdalena.

But, if the scale and complexity of the English suites can make them seem less intimate and less instantly alluring, they soon repay the slightly greater effort involved in getting to know them. The greatness, or at any rate the grandness, of the music derives principally from the fact that each suite begins with an imposing, challenging, severely contrapuntal prelude, a feature Bach chose not to employ in the lighter French suites.

With their emphasis on minor keys – only two of the six are in the major – the suites do tend to sound deeply serious, dark-toned, sometimes more mathematical than emotional. The very substantial prelude to the D minor suite pursues its course pensively at first, as if the composer is gradually feeling his way into the music. Hesitating at times on what sounds like the brink of a dance, he eventually takes the plunge. The effect is rhythmically rousing, though perhaps in a somewhat grumpy sort of way, shot through with moments of lightness where the weighty textures suddenly clear.

This, so far, is the assertive rather than the poetic side of Bach. But the following allemande, or German dance, is more relaxed. So is the succeeding courante, which flows rather than flashes. The music here seems to be preparing itself for the ensuing sarabande, which forms the beautiful, brooding heart of the work, every note, chord, decoration, small silence perfectly placed on its way to what comes next.

The two gavottes are a delight, real highlights of Bach's gavotte output, the first in the minor, the second entrancingly in the major, before the first repeats itself. These are moments of good cheer in a predominantly uncheerful work, and they extend into the robust vigour of the final gigue.

The minor-key intensity of this D minor suite is rivalled by that of the G minor, No. 3 in the series. A feature of these works, as of all such suites by Bach, is that each of them is based in the key of its opening movement. What starts in G minor, in other words, sustains that key, however dark its tonality, and however much it modulates. The prelude to the G minor suite, a relentless, rather motoric study in triple time, thus provides a powerful taste of things to come, with an obsessive, repeated-note figure which triggers each appearance of the running line on which the music is based.

The proportions of the succeeding allemande and courante are more in keeping with what we think of as dance suites; but the sarabande is very slow and special, complete with a 'double', or variation, in which the music's sombre, groping harmonies are laden with richly expressive ornamentation. The succeeding triptych of gavottes – the last a repeat of the first, with a musette (or bagpipe episode) planted in the middle – lighten the atmosphere with their perky, angular tunes, succinct interplay of minor and major keys, and touches of drone bass. The suite ends with a galloping gigue.

Works such as these demand a master performer, and the Canadian pianist Glenn Gould has been one of the few to truly meet their challenge. Almost alone among modern performers, he rejoiced in the fact that Bach's keyboard music was meant to be played in solitude or, at most, in the presence of just one or two listeners. Gould, whose gradual withdrawal from public life has been the subject of books, was the ideal person to explore the private side of Bach, playing the music in his personal bunker to an audience of microphones.

Thus did he achieve his own twentieth-century equivalent of Bach's original intentions, and pursued it more and more rigorously after his career as a concert-hall performer ceased to interest him. The occasion when Leonard Bernstein publicly disclaimed responsibility for a performance of Brahms's First Piano Concerto with Gould as soloist was an act of sabotage which must surely have formed a turning point in Gould's progress towards privacy.

Today the jury remains divided over whether Gould was a genius or eccentric, though he was clearly both. The interplay of mind, fingers and sense of adventure made him a Bach performer par excellence. Even his tendency to hum along with the music formed part of the privacy, which those who eavesdrop on his recordings must take or leave. But, if you can take it, these are enthralling performances which revel in the notes of Bach's music, examining them, articulating them and making of them an experience entirely personal and, for all its idiosyncrasy, entirely Bachian (Sony Classical SM2K52606).

Eight

1722 AND 1740
THE WELL-TEMPERED CLAVIER,
BOOKS 1 AND 2, BWV 846–93

The two volumes of Bach's forty-eight Preludes and Fugues — whether known as *Das Wohltemperirte Clavier* or, as in Britain, simply as 'the Forty-Eight' — are among the supreme demonstrations of his greatness and fecundity of invention. To play them as an entity is possible, though hardly advisable, even if there have been performers capable of tackling such a four-hour marathon — and from memory, too. To play twenty-four or even twelve of them in a single sitting calls for a player not only physically and mentally resourceful but also with the alertness of an air-traffic controller at a major international airport.

As a marathon more challenging than the six cello suites or sextet of works for solo violin, it clearly has its temptations. Yet on the whole, even if your name is Yo-Yo Ma, Itzhak Perlman or Andras Schiff, such temptations are to be resisted. As Alfred Brendel remarks in his wisdom-laden conversation book, *The Veil of Music*, there are 'gourmands of music' and 'gourmets of music'. The first, he says, cannot get enough of it; the second prefer to enjoy beauty in measured quantities. Some of the most entrancing performances of these pieces in recent times have undoubtedly been the isolated preludes and fugues which, for a spell, were presented around midnight in ten-minute close-up on BBC television.

The best way to savour the Forty-Eight tends to be in conjunction with something else. Three preludes and fugues could form an apt prologue to a selection of Bach's partitas. A further three could introduce an evening of English suites. This, surely, is the way to do it. Only a gourmand could complain of an insufficiency of contrasts, or of a failure to communicate the sheer scale of Bach's two vast volumes. What we can learn from a gifted Bachian's choice of pieces is why he or she has chosen these ones and not others, why they are being played in a certain order, and whether the decisions sound spontaneous, the performances perhaps even improvisatory, or meticulously pre-planned. The permutations, after all, are immense, and they are lost if the player, as happens often enough, devotes an entire recital to one or the other of the volumes of the Forty-Eight.

The complete ninety-six pieces were not, in any case, intended as a marathon, though one of the things we know about Bach as a composer and performer is that he was by no means uncompetitive. The music was written and assembled over a long period – Volume One, off and on, took some fifteen years to complete, and a further twenty years passed before the even more challenging Volume Two was ready, though Bach himself seems not necessarily to have considered it a follow-up to Volume One.

During the intervening period, he wrote much other music. Why did the preludes and fugues so preoccupy him? The main reason, though it may not seem so important now, was to make a thorough and methodical case for 'equal temperament', which was why he compiled them under the title of *The Well-Tempered* [or 'well-tuned'] *Clavier* – a well-tempered name which, in the twentieth century, inspired a witty book by the American humorist, S. J. Perlman, called *The Ill-Tempered Clavichord*.

Yet the meaning of Bach's title, except to connoisseurs, is by no means clear. It does not specify any particular instrument, 'clavier' meaning, simply, 'keyboard'. For domestic performances, in Bach's time, a small, light-toned clavichord might have seemed appropriate, with the advantage that it was unlikely to disturb the neighbours.

It would not, however, have conveyed the range and colour of these pieces. The harpsichord has always seemed the definitive instrument for them, though there is a difference between Wanda Landowska's mighty armour-plated harpsichord and one of the more perfumed instruments employed by more recent performers. But the harpsichord, even Landowska's, is not an invincible Bachian tool. Increasingly, the grand piano, small or large, has nudged its way into the Bach repertoire, contributing – via the hands of Edwin Fischer or Rosalyn Tureck, Glenn

Gould or Andras Schiff, Angela Hewitt or Till Ferner – a less spiky beauty of tone and a greater, weightier wealth of expression to the challenges and the ways of performance supplied or implied by the music.

The 'well-tempered' element of the title derives from what was once the music's major, if seemingly somewhat didactic, aim, which was to champion the development of equal temperament and spread its gospel. The system of tuning keyboard instruments was a controversial subject in Bach's time. The old system, as H. C. Colles, editor of the third and fourth editions of *Grove's Dictionary*, pointed out, was a mixed blessing; it made the instruments sound beautifully in tune in certain keys, but unbearable in others. The new system meant compromising on pitch, in that the notes F sharp and G flat, for example, would sound exactly the same as each other (which they would not quite do on a violin or cello), but had the benefit of laying open the entire circle of major and minor keys to the composer and performer.

As the title page confirms, Bach completed the first part of his eloquent musical manifesto in 1722, his ground-plan having been to start in C major and work upwards through every major and minor key. Then, having done it in Volume One, he did it again in Volume Two, with no dilution of inspiration. The pieces are no mere exercises, though they are often enough employed as teaching pieces. They are the fountainhead of all subsequent keyboard music, and an inexhaustible comfort and pleasure to perform – Donald Francis Tovey, Edinburgh's wise musical essayist, decreed that people who were capable of playing them should do so for an hour every day of their lives.

And they encompass every facet of Bach's musical personality: serene and sombre, intimate and majestic, racy and intense, spiritual and brilliant. They are also virtually indestructible, having been sumptuously orchestrated by Stokowski and others, transformed into jazz by Jacques Loussier and others (no difficult feat this, for some of them are jazzy already), played on every conceivable form of keyboard and, in the case of the very first prelude, metamorphosed by Gounod into his sugary *Ave Maria*.

Later composers have responded to them with similar works of their own – Chopin with his Twenty-four Preludes, Debussy with his two books of preludes and Shostakovich with his Twenty-four Preludes and Fugues. Nor was Bach, when he completed his forty-eighth fugue, finished with the idea. Approaching the subject from a different though no less comprehensive standpoint, he was still at work on *The Art of Fugue* at the time of his death.

Joseph Kerman, that most vivid of musicologists, has called Bach's preludes and fugues a 'limited, specialised, precious repertoire', which is why they retain something of their original privacy even while attracting large, eager modern audiences. Charles Rosen, the American scholar-pianist, claims that a Bach keyboard fugue 'can be fully understood only by the one who plays it, not only heard but felt through the muscles and nerves'. This may seem to be taking didacticism rather far, yet its truth is unassailable – though happily, even if you cannot play them, it is still possible to get much out of listening to them.

At one time, this would happen on a one-to-one basis, the relationship between the performer at the keyboard and the solitary listener in the armchair never closer. Today, the combination of iPod and headphones supplies an even closer connection, to the extent that the performance seems to be taking place inside your brain. If this is what you desire, then Kenneth Gilbert's constantly illuminating harpsichord version of Volume One, recorded in the Musée de Chartres, is the perfect starting point (Archiv Produktion Blue 474-221-2ABL), just as Rosalyn Tureck's piano version of both volumes supplies the complete picture in tones gloriously unhurried, thoughtful and sublime (DG 463 305-2GH4).

Tureck's is *The Well-Tempered Clavier* treated as a probing, philosophical quest. Till Fellner's is the opposite, a smooth, sensuous unfurling of the music, with sudden jolts of electricity, left-hand pulsations, light-and-dark harmonies. This young Austrian pianist is a pupil of Alfred Brendel, and it shows (ECM New Series 1853-4).

Nine

1723?
CONCERTO FOR TWO VIOLINS AND STRINGS IN D MINOR, BWV 1043

Vivace   Largo ma non tanto   Allegro

Among Bach's concertos for two or more solo instruments, the D minor for two violins and the C minor for oboe and violin are works of a very special sort: vivid, varied, on-spinning, filled with melodic and contrapuntal impetus. Edinburgh's tireless musical essayist, Donald Francis Tovey, hailed them as twin brothers, which was not just a polite way of saying that the one was a copy of the other. Their facial resemblances, including a passage shared more or less by each of their slow movements, are obvious enough. Their most significant common feature, however, is the fact that, like other Bach concertos, they are conspicuously the offspring of Antonio Vivaldi (1678–1741), a composer accused far more often of writing the same work over and over and over again.

Bach discovered Vivaldi's concertos at a crucial moment in his career, when he was ready to turn away from German tradition and draw inspiration from what was happening around the same time in Italy. Without ever crossing the Alps, as Handel in his prentice years was happy to do, Bach stayed in his study, privately copying out and transcribing many Vivaldi concertos for his own benefit. Their influence on his music was profound. Out went concertos and orchestral suites written in a multiplicity of movements. In came the three-movement format favoured by the Italian, and celebrated in our own time by the Edinburgh writer Ron Butlin in his witty book of surrealist short stories entitled *Vivaldi and the Number Three*.

Like Vivaldi's concertos, Bach's for two violins in D minor is succinct, circling, vivaciously rhythmic, indelibly melodious, and dependent on constant contrast between the two soloists and the rest of the strings. Yet the effect, for all its Italian leanings, is unmistakably Bachian, just as it is in those works which Bach, as part of his development as a composer of concertos, based directly on already-existent music by Vivaldi and others. Not until Stravinsky did something similar two centuries later would a great composer make another great composer's music so completely his own.

This, then, was Italian music cultivated to a point where it ceased to be Italian and changed into something else – in a word something German, but German with an Italian twist, and German with the genius of Johann

Sebastian Bach to galvanise it. By the time he composed this work, he had escaped from his residency at Weimar, where he had developed his flair for organ music and church cantatas, and where a statue – not much else of note – now commemorates the nine not wholly happy years he spent there. The names people came to associate with Weimar were Goethe, Schiller, Liszt, and Walter Gropius's Bauhaus movement in art and architecture, rather than the less flamboyant Bach; and it was these varied geniuses who sprang primarily to mind when Weimar became European City of Culture in 1999.

The city's proximity to Buchenwald concentration camp was something it had by then lived down. But Bach, long before, had shown characteristic disrespect for the place when, having had enough of it, he abruptly decided to pack his bags and move elsewhere. Anticipating a dictum which would be voiced two centuries later by Lord Hill as chairman of ITV – 'never show the slightest twinge of loyalty to your current employer' – he slighted the Weimar court (which deemed him, in any case, an insubordinate schemer) and accepted an offer from the genial Prince Leopold of Anhalt-Cothen to go and work for him.

In response, and in revenge, the Duke of Weimar had Bach arrested and jailed for a month. Then, having been made to eat humble pie, the stubborn composer was released because – as the duke unwillingly put it – he 'could not be forced to stay'. Four days later (his second wife,

Anna Magdalena, having attended to the drudgery of the removal during his imprisonment), he arrived triumphantly in Cothen with a better salary and the financial enticement of renting a room in his house to his musicians to rehearse in. Nice work, he might have said, if you can get it. Bach, for all the dryness of his reputation, was an astute operator, even if he missed the occasional trick.

Cothen proved a very different musical environment from Weimar. Being a Calvinist stronghold, it forbade Bach to produce music for performance in church but made up for this by encouraging him to compose the secular instrumental works – concertos, suites, sonatas – for which he would later become even more famed. Among them was the D minor concerto for two violins, fondly known as the 'Double', which he wrote sometime between 1717 and 1723, though it has never been established exactly when. Later, in Leipzig, he would write another version of it for two harpsichords; but the marvellous string original was never in danger of being usurped by its subsequent rival. It has deservedly remained the *ne plus ultra* of all Bach's (indeed, anybody's) works for string orchestra.

In standard baroque fashion, the first movement delivers its main theme without preamble. What is not so standard is the sheer intensity of this fine, driving melody, played first by the orchestra before being taken up by the soloists. To speak of its electrifying energy, as at least one commentator has done, may seem to be going a bit far in Bachian concerto terms, yet that is what it surely possesses. With the entry of the soloists, one after the other, the music becomes a play of voice against voice, in which the rest of the strings join.

This contrapuntal interaction, vivacious in the first movement, becomes sweet and serene in the second, whose swaying phrases are kept buoyant by Bach's request that they be played *largo ma non tanto* – not too slowly. Here, the music conveys a soft rapture which is conspicuously out of keeping with the idea of Bach as a stern contrapuntist, but which is thoroughly attuned to the other, more romantic side of his musical persona. But, just as the magic thread of the main theme begins to give the impression that it could unwind for ever, the music halts and gives way to a finale whose tension exceeds anything which has already been heard in the first movement.

The most useful – and, as it happens, the two best – recordings of the double violin concerto in D minor are ones which also incorporate the C minor concerto for oboe and violin and the pair of masterpieces, in A minor and E major, for solo violin. Of these, the one by Arthur Grumiaux, the distinguished Belgian, and Herman Krebbers, former leader of Amsterdam's Concertgebouw Orchestra, is a long-established classic, with the gifted Heinz Holliger as solo oboist in the C minor work (Philips 420 700-2PSL).

Grumiaux, though no modern authenticist, was a fine and deeply serious player, heard at his best in this 1970s disc. For sounds which are more genuinely and exhilaratingly baroque, however, look no further than the recording by Rachel Podger and Andrew Manze with the Academy of Ancient Music – it is a model of its kind and alert to every nuance of the music (Harmonia Mundi HMU90 7155).

Ten

1726
CANTATA NO. 170, *VERGNÜGTE RUH*, BWV 170

'On August 9 the Cantorate test was passed by Mr Telemann, yet after he had received an increase of a few hundred thaler in Hamburg he withdrew his application. On February 7 the following year Mr Sebastian Bach passed the Cantorate test.' From these perfunctory words can be deciphered the facts behind one of the great moments in European musical history. Georg Philipp Telemann's application for the job of cantor at St Thomas's, Leipzig, had resulted in his accepting a better offer from elsewhere. Only after Telemann and a second contender had backed out was the post finally offered to the 39-year-old Johann Sebastian Bach.

This very modern-sounding process of negotiation reached its completion in 1724. The outcome of Telemann's refusal, as we now know, was the composition by Bach of 200 cantatas, two versions of a great *Magnificat*, two magisterial *Passion*s, a B minor Mass and a *Christmas*

Oratorio. What the similarly prolific Telemann might have bestowed on Leipzig was church music more obviously charming than Bach's, but 'inferior' in the sense that Salieri was inferior to Mozart. True, it did not seem so at the time, and Telemann was in any case a good, now rather underrated composer. Bach, on the other hand, was in 1724 the 'mediocre' composer who proceeded to cling to his job for the remaining twenty-seven years of his life.

Today, we cling to what remain of his church cantatas, admiring them for their beauty, resourcefulness and intensity of expression. We wish that still more of them could have survived, and recognise them as not at all the weekly penance which some members of the original congregation (stepping outside for the equivalent of a smoke while the music was in progress) clearly considered them to be. Far from immediately asserting themselves as masterpieces which would endure from one year to the next, Bach's cantatas – deemed severe, contrapuntal, more often depressing than uplifting – were lucky to outlive their first performance.

Things are different now, and nothing less than rapt attention seems fit for the Cantata No. 170, whatever people thought of it on the sixth Sunday after Trinity in July 1726. Its five movements – three arias interwoven with two recitatives – can be said to possess an operatic eloquence, if it is possible to associate such a thing with Bach, a non-operatic composer if ever there was one. Yet these arias, in which the subject of mortality is approached from three different angles, are conspicuously heartfelt, wonderfully contrasted, drawing gentle instrumental colours from a deliberately restricted palette in which a dark-toned oboe d'amore plays the most expressive of roles. If this music is non-operatic, then so much the worse for opera.

Though good performances of *Vergnügte Ruh* can be found among the ever-lengthening recorded collections of Bach cantatas, two versions on single discs stand out from the crowd. Both are by fine period ensembles and both feature distinguished counter-tenors, heard to high advantage in this alto music. James Bowman's intensity of timbre, combined with the plangent tones of the King's Consort, provides ample proof that Bach's cantatas, whatever their first listeners may have thought of them, can speak eloquently to us across the centuries. The Cantata No. 169, *Gott soll allein mein Herze haben* ('God alone shall have my heart'), written around the same time, and the much earlier Cantata No. 54, dating from the composer's Weimar period, complete the disc and confirm that liking a Bach cantata is far from being just a matter of luck, and that coming upon a cantata which you do not already know is almost invariably a revelation.

Recorded by Hyperion (CDA 66326) with appropriate intimacy, this is a disc to cherish. It is challenged, however, by Andreas Scholl's account of two of the same cantatas (Nos 54 and 170) by the Collegium Vocale Orchestra under Philippe Herreweghe, this time with the concerto-like Cantata No. 35, complete with obbligato organ, as ballast (Harmonia Mundi HMC90 1644).

Eleven

1728
Partita No. 4 in D major, BWV 828

Ouverture   Allemande   Courante   Aria

Sarabande   Menuet   Gigue

For many listeners, Bach is a composer who always looked grim. His face frowns out of pictures reproduced on book covers and record sleeves, evidence of his attitude to church councillors and civic bureaucrats who had the temerity to cross him. Yet the music so often seems to contradict the man that, if we were deprived of the portraits, we would assume him to have been thoroughly romantic and vivacious.

The Partita No. 4 in D major, one of a set of six keyboard works written in his early forties, is a case in point. True, it is filled with what might seem to be intimidatingly baroque counterpoint – 'and Protestant counterpoint at that', as Sir Thomas Beecham, a dedicated Handelian, once caustically complained of Bach's music. But the harmonies of the allemande which forms this partita's elaborately melodic second movement tell a different story.

An allemande – a French word for a German dance – is one of the traditional movements of a baroque suite. Usually described as being moderately paced and laid out in two sections, each of them repeated, it may not seem to provide the prospect of a great emotional experience. Yet that is what this particular allemande is. A dance it may be, but it is a dance transformed into fantasy, something that does not sound like a dance at all, music entirely pensive, probing, mysterious, rather slower than 'moderately paced', roaming through a world of feeling that never releases its grip on the listener's imagination.

What does this music mean? How did it get there? Whatever the answer, its effect on Bach himself was clearly to inspire in him not only the longest, most intense movement in any of his six keyboard partitas, but also one that grows increasingly rich and profound as it proceeds, with a melodic line which slowly meanders over a smooth accompaniment. Coming just after a characteristic baroque overture (consisting of a jerkily majestic prelude followed by a swinging fugue) and just before a fleet-fingered courante, full of rhythmic legerdemain, it is positioned to make its maximum expressive impact, as Bach obviously intended.

Yet it does not reduce the other movements to mere baroque baggage. The aria that follows the mercurial ascents and descents of the courante is a masterpiece of Bachian wit, a scherzo ahead of its time. The slow sarabande, with its questioning opening phrase, takes up where the allemande left off. The minuet and gigue are dance movements of the most rhythmically ingenious sort, the first of them sounding like a greatly speeded-up sarabande, the second a circus-ring marvel of contrapuntal juggling.

In terms of sheer expressiveness, the huge allemande from the D major Partita towers over everything else in these works. In other respects, Bach's six keyboard partitas may seem, at first impression, structurally much of a muchness, in that each has six or seven movements, mingling vivacity with repose. Or – putting it another way – each combines baroque dances with matter more severely contrapuntal. Each begins with some form of prelude and ends with a scintillating gigue. Each contains a grandly expressive sarabande. Each has a special point of focus, which varies from work to work in scale and feeling.

Yet the works fall into two distinct categories, the three in major keys possessing an airiness greatly in contrast with the power, darker colouring and emotional intensity of the three in the minor. Johann Forkel, Bach's early biographer, declared that anybody with the six partitas under his fingers 'could make his way with success' in the world of music. But how many people had them under their fingers? How many, for that matter, had been attracted to, or repelled by, Bach's standard description of them as *Keyboard Practice*?

As more than one Bach authority has reminded us, however, the term 'keyboard' practice did not imply scales and arpeggios, much though

Bach employed these in his music. What it meant was that it put into practice Bach's perception of various musical styles and techniques, and that – as he charmingly added – it was 'prepared for the refreshment of the souls of music-lovers'.

Above all, though Bach did not need to say so, each of the six works has its own personality, which is why they form such an exhilarating, enticing collection, containing material to match all our moods. The tension of the E minor and D minor partitas speaks for itself, but so does the benign beauty of the B flat major partita which, for some listeners, is the jewel in the crown. Bach composed it in 1726, some three years after completing the first volume of *The Well-Tempered Clavier*. Describing it initially as a keyboard 'exercise', he published it separately from the five other works which would later be assembled alongside it. This was to become a time of high productivity for him, during which he wrote some of his most famous keyboard works, including the *Italian Concerto* and the *Goldberg Variations*.

In the first three movements, the emphasis is on gently flowing major-key lines rather than on the more restless rhythms which are so much a feature of Bach's minor-key music. Yet there is plenty of power to drive the gigue-like courante through its paces before the arrival of the slow-moving sarabande, always a moment of haunting expressiveness in Bach's suites. In this one, with its tenderly hesitant phrases and exquisite embellishments, he does not let us down. The contrasted minuets are light and charming, and the gigue, relentlessly cross-handed, is a pulsating tour de force.

This, thanks to its sheer allure, is the partita to which performers often give pride of place in their repertoire. Piotr Anderszewski, the fleet-fingered young Polish pianist, justifiably makes it the climax of his recording of three of these works, treating the final gigue almost as if it were a toccata finale by Prokofiev. The A minor and E minor partitas, however, prove no mere curtain-raisers. For anyone wanting a selection of these works, rather than a complete set, Anderszewski's is the one to have (Virgin 5 45526-2).

Trevor Pinnock's millennial recording of the entire cycle, however, is in a very special class, a true celebration of the year 2000. Employing a modern American copy of a Hemsch harpsichord, he produces timbres of the utmost expressiveness, delivering the allemande from the D major Partita with timeless beauty and perception. This in itself would make the set worth acquiring, but his mastery of style, pace, colour and feeling is so abundant that the music sings from start to finish (Hanssler Classic 92 115).

Twelve

1729
ST MATTHEW PASSION, BWV 244

Baroque musical pietism, in its darkest form, is about thorns, whips, torture and trickling blood rather than melodious abstractions. So we should expect a work such as Bach's *St Matthew Passion* to be disturbing as well as uplifting, its performers drawing attention to its harshness as well as its beauty, to its images of pain and cruelty as well as its gentleness, to its urgency and violence as well as its compassion. In these respects, the *St Matthew Passion*, like the earlier, shorter *St John*, is a musical fresco almost operatic in its intensity and directness, its cast of singers headed by a tenor Evangelist, who narrates the story with eloquent interjections from a baritone Jesus.

In supporting roles are two maids, two false witnesses, Pilate's wife, Peter, Judas, Pilate, Caiaphas, two priests, plus four or five expressive soloists for arias – a possible total of eighteen voices, though Bach himself, choosing them from his choristers at the Thomas Kirk in Leipzig, could raise only seventeen he considered trustworthy. Modern concert performances, by doubling roles for the sake of economy and intimacy, do it with fewer, though there is still scope, albeit diminishing, for the magisterial versions of Bach, with armies of choristers and star-spangled soloists, once favoured by Otto Klemperer, Herbert von Karajan, Willem Mengelberg and other conductors with a flair for the monolithic (though in Karajan's case merely smooth and sleepy) approach.

Either way, the work offers potent crowd scenes, arias with plangent instrumental accompaniments, recitatives which not only tell the story in keen, concise tones but also say something about the character of the Evangelist himself and about his emotional responses to every detail of Christ's demise. Bach composed no operas; but the musical qualities of the *St Matthew Passion*, with its dramatic interruptions – the huge shout of 'Barabbas!' (which can reverberate, it is said, for as long as fifteen seconds in big-scale London performances at St Paul's Cathedral) being only the most sensational of many – and its passages of lengthy operatic contemplation, are those of a man who might have written masterpieces for the stage, and who, in a sense, did so: Bach's theatre was his church. The operatic aspects of the *St Matthew Passion* (for which he was severely chided by at least one of his contemporaries) are nevertheless no excuse for modern attempts to stage the music as an opera. The point about the *St Matthew Passion* is that it is not an opera.

The work marks the climax of a musical tradition which had begun years earlier. The story of Christ's suffering and crucifixion was recited in church during the services for Holy Week at least as early as the fourth century AD. By the tenth century, musical settings of the Passion, with plainsong, were being regularly performed. When Martin Luther reformed the German church service in 1522, placing more emphasis on music and on the congregation's participation in the performance, the way was open for composers to treat the Passion as an increasingly eloquent music drama which would find its nineteenth-century destination in Wagner's *Parsifal*. Heinrich Schütz's settings, inspired by his visits to Italy in the early seventeenth century (when he heard the music of Monteverdi), were the most theatrically expressive Passion music written before Bach.

Bach himself composed at least four, possibly five, *Passions*, though only the *Matthew* and *John* have survived complete. Material from a missing *St Mark Passion* has been tracked down in other works by Bach. The authenticity of the *St Luke Passion*, of which a score exists in Germany, has been subject to doubt. The *St John Passion* had its first performance in Leipzig in 1723 or 1724. Critical listeners have sometimes reckoned it to be a 'preparation' for the *Matthew*, deeming the more famous and longer work, dating from 1729, to be automatically the greater and more subtle score.

More recently, however, the *St John Passion* has been hailed as no less masterly, complementing the *Matthew* and being written with a terseness which counterbalances the *Matthew*'s gloomy grandeur. This brevity was brought about partly by Bach's shunning of all but the most essential solo arias – the *Matthew*, with inspiration running high, has more than twice the number. As a result, the miniature score of the *St Matthew Passion* runs to 336 pages, as compared with 190 for the *St John*.

In each work, the text is based on the Gospel narrative in German, interwoven with contemplative chorale verses, original texts for the opening and closing choruses, and texts for arias and ariosos drawn mostly from the Passion libretto written by Barthold Brockes of Hamburg in 1712. The short chorales were originally aimed at congregational participation, though today's 'authentic' performances tend deliberately, and for obvious reasons, to overlook this aspect of performances in Bach's time. The orchestration is for woodwind, strings and continuo, with special obbligato parts for solo instruments, including the deep-toned oboe d'amore ('oboe of love'), the even deeper oboe da caccia ('hunting oboe'), and viola da gamba, a forerunner of the cello, so called because the player rests it on his knee (*gamba*) rather than on the floor.

At its first performance, beginning at 1:45pm on 15 April 1729, the *St Matthew Passion* formed part of a church service incorporating several separate chorales, a motet and a forty-five-minute sermon which divided the two parts of the almost four-hour *Passion*. But there was more to it than that. As the English Bach scholar, Peter Williams, has harshly explained, the period when the composer was working on his *St John* and *St Matthew Passion*s was a time when public executions in Leipzig were fairly regular, the whole patrolled by the army, led by the clergy, and not least accompanied to the place of execution ('outside the city walls, as in Jerusalem') by the choristers. 'And these', as Williams adds, 'were under the municipal director of music, Johann Sebastian Bach.'

The authorities issued news-sheets explaining what the condemned had done and what the method of death was to be – the sword for women, hanging for Jews, the wheel for the worst offenders. 'I think something of the intensity of Bach's Passions is lost as we sit silently listening to them,' says Williams, 'with knowledge neither of such things nor of the usual Good Friday traditions.'

With that as background, Bach's *St Matthew Passion* must originally have seemed not only sombre but also cruelly topical. Purely by musical standards, however, the first performance must have formed a long Good Friday, made to seem even longer by the variable quality of the performance, which drew caustic comments from the composer in his personal memorandum. No doubt today's neo-authentic performances would have infuriated him likewise – Bach was nothing if not irascible – though he could hardly have failed to appreciate their technical finesse.

For ourselves, if we are broad-minded enough, we can savour the dynamism brought to the music by modern conductors of the calibre of John Eliot Gardiner and Paul McCreesh without dismissing the weighty grandeur of Willem Mengelberg's famous Palm Sunday performance (preserved on disc) which he gave in Amsterdam just before the outbreak of the Second World War. Though its stylistic shortcomings today speak for themselves, its emotional veracity sweeps all before it. If Bach needs a great conductor, and there are many reasons for disputing this, then Mengelberg was as great as they came.

In Mengelberg's hands, as the English composer-critic Robin Holloway has pointed out in a masterly essay on this historic performance, Christ's institution of the Eucharist is made to sound 'beautiful in Bach's setting beyond creed or sacrament'. Likewise, the aria of meditation on Peter's betraying his master is the 'supreme expression anywhere of contrition and self-reproach'; and the tiny chorus, testifying after Jesus's death that 'Truly this was the son of God', encapsulates in a few simple chords an utterance 'as profound as religion itself'.

Today's performers bring out other aspects of the music – its dancing rhythms, even in the great opening and closing choruses (the latter indeed based on a sarabande Bach had composed for solo keyboard) and the intimacy which can be achieved when the work is voiced by just a small handful of singers. Although, as a result, the music may be expected to lack ballast, it is only in weak performances or in poor acoustics that it does so. In good performances, and in suitable surroundings, the stereophonic double choruses at the start of Part One, where the words 'Behold!' and 'Behold what?' swing between one group of singers and the other, lose nothing in their effect. The eruption of the thunder-and-lightning chorus gains in swiftness, and the shout of 'Barabbas' may lack weight of numbers but is no less ferocious in its blood-lust.

The recitatives and arias, however, are what gain above all from such small-scale but big-hearted performances, especially if 'Erbarme dich' ('Have mercy'), with its violin obbligato, is sung by the right mezzo-soprano or counter-tenor in tones poignant yet not bereft of sweetness. Among several excellent modern recordings, the one by Paul McCreesh and his Gabrieli Players is the most pared down but by no means the least passionate, with Mark Padmore as an eloquent Evangelist and Magdalena Kozena outstanding among the soloists. Recorded in 2002, this is a lucid, fast-paced, thoroughly dramatic rendering of the Easter story (Archiv 474 200-2AH2).

From Sir John Eliot Gardiner with his Monteverdi Choir and English Baroque Soloists (Archiv DG 427 648-2), and from Nikolaus Harnoncourt in the second of his two recordings with the Vienna Concentus Musicus (Teldec 8573-81036-2), we get a similarly direct, unflagging approach to the music, each reflecting the personality of its conductor, and wonderfully delivered by each team of voices and instrumentalists. Christophe Prégardien and Matthias Goerne, as Evangelist and Jesus, are major assets of the Harnoncourt set, though Anthony Rolfe Johnson and Andreas Schmidt on the Gardiner are scarcely inferior.

In comparison, Masaaki Suzuki's Japanese approach to this monument of German music may sound a little over-manicured, but is certainly very lovely, if that is what you expect a performance of the *St Matthew Passion* to be (BIS CD 1000/1002). Frans Bruggen's performance with the Netherlands Chamber Chorus and Orchestra is similarly intimate but more assertive – and you can buy it at bargain price (Philips 473 262-3).

Thirteen

1731
ORCHESTRAL SUITE NO. 3 IN D MAJOR, BWV 1068

Ouverture   Air   Gavottes 1 and 2   Bourrée   Gigue

Bach's four orchestral suites, or 'overtures', are big, demonstrative works which great conductors — none of them greater at one time than Wilhelm Furtwängler — still consider to lie within the stylistic range of big symphony orchestras. They do not really, of course, and Bach never intended them to do so, for the simple reason that the symphony orchestra had not been invented when he wrote them. Yet there is something about them which lends itself to large-scale orchestral treatment in a way that the Brandenburg concertos, which employ similarly varied and imaginative instrumental colouring, do not. As entertainment music for the general public, rather than court music for a select audience, Bach's suites have their own role to play in his output, and (like Handel's *Water*

Music and *Fireworks Music*, to which they bear a certain resemblance) they play it very successfully.

Yet there is no evidence that they were written for some special reason or ceremonial occasion, that they date from the same time and the same place, or that they were intended to form some sort of entity in the manner of the Brandenburgs. The long-held assumption that they belong to Bach's Cothen period, when he was composing secular music for instruments rather than sacred music for voices, now seems at best only partly true. Two of them, Nos 1 and 4, are considered to have Cothen connections and to have been written as chamber music for private performance there. But the Second and Third suites, misleadingly numbered, seem both to have been composed later, probably for Collegium Musicum events in Leipzig, which Bach – by then cantor of St Thomas's – ran as a sort of secular sideline.

Certainly, these are deservedly the most popular of the four works, melodically more memorable, instrumentally more scintillating than the others, with a mercurial flute part in No. 2, sonorous trumpets and drums in No. 3. These lusty instruments, however, do not intrude upon the haunting, sweet-spun thread of string tone which forms the latter suite's slow movement, known (for no convincing reason) as the 'Air on the G string' and often performed out of context. Structured in two short sections, each of them played twice, and underpinned by the gentle pulse of a 'walking' bass line, this is Bach at his simplest and softest, all the better for being heard immediately after the grandeur of the opening overture.

The latter movement – which Bach entitled 'ouverture' in the original, signifying that he wrote it in a French rather than German manner – is what gives this suite and its three companion pieces their formal name. Not only is it the biggest movement but it is also the most elaborate, with an imposing slow introduction, incorporating jerky baroque rhythms and trumpet intrusions. By the time the fugal central section is reached, the music has swung from D major into the related key of A, with trumpet tone again strongly projected and edgy oboes in the background. The whole effect is full of splendour, the pace now much faster, the violin part being marked with the indication *viste*, which is old French for 'vite' or 'quick'. Once this has run its course, the movement is buttressed by the return of the slow introduction in the home key of D major.

The succeeding air, in spite of its 'G string' nickname, is also in D, its music sublime enough to survive all attempts to alter it, sentimentalise it or trivialise it. Ideally, it should move rather faster than tradition dictates. Then, as in the three other suites, come a few French dances – a pair of gavottes (the first with a tune which is turned upside-down in its second half), a quick bourrée, and a racy gigue in which the trumpets are exuberantly exploited. The movements never outstay their welcome. Their rhythms are richly and elegantly French, their whole effect poised and sophisticated.

As recently as the 2004 Edinburgh Festival, the Suite No. 2 was being toured by the famed Leipzig Gewandhaus Orchestra, one of Europe's grandest symphony orchestras, clearly intent on trading (albeit with little stylistic authority) on that city's Bach associations. Yet, alongside works by Beethoven and Hindemith, the homogenised sonorities obtained by the conductor Herbert Blomstedt did not seem out of place, even if they were no closer to Bach than Sir Hamilton Harty's obese version of the *Water Music* was to Handel. What they lacked was the sharp tang of authenticity now provided by small specialist bands such as Musica Antiqua Köln, the Orchestra of the Age of the Enlightenment, or the English Baroque Soloists.

For an impression of what the music is really about, the recordings by these groups are of the keenest interest, especially as they each include all four suites (plus extras) in performances of the utmost refinement. Reinhard Goebel and his Cologne-based outfit approach each work with a colour, personality and abrasiveness much to be savoured in these pieces (Archiv 415 671-2). Frans Bruggen and the OAE, in comparison, sound lighter and friendlier, though disappointingly prone to omit repeated sections (Philips 442 151-2PH2). For sheer zip and freshness, however, John Eliot Gardiner and the English Baroque Soloists are (like America's Boston Baroque Orchestra) hard to beat (Warner Ultima 0927-41387-2).

Fourteen

1733
MAGNIFICAT IN D MAJOR, BWV 243

Magnificat	Et exsultavit	Quia respexit	Omnes generationes
Quia fecit mihi magna		Et misericordia	Fecit potentiam
Deposuit potentes		Esurientes	Suscepit Israel
Sicut locutus			Gloria

Sir Donald Tovey, as usual, had a phrase for it. Bach's *Magnificat*, claimed Edinburgh University's resident musical essayist, is one of the composer's 'most comprehensively representative works'. More arguable, he said, was whether it was a representative setting of the Song of the Virgin Mary – which is what a *Magnificat* is meant to be – or whether the question was irrelevant to listeners who simply love the music.

Attitudes to Bach have changed since Tovey's day, but the above comments still hold. Nobody now would fault Bach – as Hubert Parry, composer of *Blest Pairs of Sirens*, once did – for producing an insufficiently 'feminine' *Magnificat* (what would Parry have made of Penderecki's macho modern setting?); and the score, with its splendid buttress-like opening and closing choruses framing a wealth of more intimate music, continues to seem not only a representative but also a wonderfully concise survey of the scope of Bach's genius.

In its original, somewhat longer version in E flat major, Bach's *Magnificat* was composed in 1723 for his first Christmas in Leipzig, with festive extra movements interpolated for the occasion. No doubt it was intended to make an impression on his new employers, as well as on the congregation at St Thomas's Church, which explains its brilliant exploitation of four or five soloists, five-part chorus, and an orchestra containing trumpets and drums as well as woodwind and strings. Quite apart from that, however, Bach seems to have been genuinely inspired by his subject, as the jubilant swing of the opening chorus confirms.

Why, then, did he choose to revise the work a decade later for a performance in Dresden, shedding the extra movements in the process and changing the key to bright D major? Partly, no doubt, because time had passed and his views on the music had changed. The sheer verve of the result, the lightning shifts of colour and mood all speak for themselves. When Bach amended one of his works, it was usually for good reason.

In its perfected version, Bach's *Magnificat* moves in a single sweep. Indeed, once it is under way, there is simply no stopping it – though Herbert von Karajan came close to doing so in a dragged-out version by the Berlin Philharmonic, with himself as one of two harpsichordists, at the 1967 Edinburgh Festival. The opening chorus (which in Edinburgh at least was dispatched with the full thrust of Arthur Oldham's festival choristers) leads straight into two short soprano arias before the chorus bursts in again with *Omnes generatione* ('All generations'), its contrapuntal outpouring of semiquavers vividly portraying a great multitude of people.

Then, after a tiny bass aria and a duet, comes a further crowd scene, *Fecit potentiam* ('He hath shown strength with his arm'), in which God is heard scattering the proud. In contrast, *Sicut locutus est* ('As he promised to our forefathers') is a minute fugue, paving the way for the splendour of the closing chorus.

Though the movements interwoven with the choruses provide space for reflection, they do not deprive the music of its momentum. The already-mentioned soprano arias, *Et exsultavit* ('And my spirit hath rejoiced') and *Quia respexit* ('For he hath regarded'), feature two different sopranos and two divergent moods, the first airy and dancelike, the second more poignant, with an exquisite obbligato for oboe d'amore, a woodwind instrument slightly lower in pitch than a standard oboe, and much loved by Bach for its mellow, expressive tone.

Quia fecit ('For he that is mighty') brings in the bass voice, very simply accompanied by continuo alone. The pastoral *Et misericordia* ('And his mercy'), another dancelike movement, sets alto and tenor voices against a flowing accompaniment of flutes and muted strings. The tenor's *Deposuit potentes* ('He hath put down the mighty') shows the more pictorial side of Bach, in that it illustrates the Latin word *deposuit* with rapid descending scales and celebrates the 'rising of the humble and meek' with rapid ascending ones.

Even more graphic, however, is the alto's *Esurientes* ('He hath filled the hungry with good things'), where, at the end, the sweetly warbling flutes are left suspended in mid-air — 'a downright practical joke', according to Tovey, who chided editors of continuo parts (or 'fillings') for adding music at this point where none was intended, the empty space being Bach's witty representation of the rich being sent away hungry.

Of all Bach's major choral works, the *Magnificat* is the one which demands of its conductor the keenest sense of pace and lightness of touch. In these respects, Paul McCreesh's racy recording with the Gabrieli Consort and Gabrieli Players is just about ideal, not least because the five soloists are also the chorus. Though some listeners might prefer weightier choral tone, the accompanying booklet makes a strong case for this 'one-to-a-part' version, and the clarity of the resultant performance certainly supports it. A side benefit of this disc is that it incorporates the *Easter Oratorio* as coupling (Archiv 469 531-2).

Fifteen

1734–5
CHRISTMAS ORATORIO, BWV 248

Just as Bach's B minor Mass is really a conflation of several other works, which he ultimately assembled into one of the greatest of all masterpieces, so the *Christmas Oratorio* is really a set of six separate cantatas, some of them incorporating revisions of previously composed material. But, just as it would be difficult now to imagine the B minor Mass split up – with the opening Kyrie performed separately, the way Bach wrote it – so we have grown used to thinking of the *Christmas Oratorio* as an entity, even though Bach composed these cantatas for performance on different days of the Christmas season. Of course, it is still perfectly possible (some would say preferable) to present them as Bach intended, and there are good reasons for doing so if a sense of Christmas over-indulgence is to be avoided.

Yet to hear them as a single sustained experience also has its advantages, for, as the Bach authority Karl Geiringer has claimed in his book on the composer, the sequence of keys and the orchestration give a kind of rondo-like character to the music which is lost if the work is divided. Three of the cantatas, including the first and last, are written in what (if the work is performed as a unity) could be called the 'home' key of D major, and are scored for what, by Bachian standards, is a large orchestra, with trumpets, drums, woodwind and strings. The drums, indeed, are given the honour of setting this great Christmas panorama on its course, with a vigorously hammering and attention-seeking solo. The other three cantatas are in different (but related) keys, and call for slightly smaller forces, with no trumpets.

The work can thereby be perceived to have an overall structure, a balance and contrast, that enables it to hang together. The unity, moreover, is not only musical but also textual; for, to quote Geiringer again: 'Sections from the New Testament (Luke 2:1, 3–21; Matthew 2:1–12) are narrated by an Evangelist, while the utterances of individual persons are entrusted to soloists, and those of a group to the chorus. The Biblical text is again and again interrupted by chorales and arias or recitative-like ariosos accompanied by the orchestra. The result is true church music, serving the purpose of edifying and uplifting the congregation.'

The approach, therefore, is similar to that of the *St Matthew Passion*, even if the effect, being joyous rather than searing, is very different. Although today we tend to listen to it as concert music, it is heard to best advantage in the atmosphere and acoustics of a suitable church. The

Russian pianist Sviatoslav Richter, in his fascinating diaries, has written that, for him, a year was sadly incomplete if he did not hear the *Christmas Oratorio* performed complete in the sort of surroundings for which it was written.

Bach's sextet of cantatas, in their final form, date from his Leipzig period, when he was firmly installed as cantor of St Thomas's and was approaching the age of 50. They were first performed at Christmas 1734 — three of them on 25, 26 and 27 December, the remainder on New Year's Day, on the following Sunday, and on the Feast of the Epiphany 1735.

In its opening chorus and its succession of recitatives, arias and chorales, the first cantata jubilantly unfolds the story of the arrival of Mary and Joseph in Bethlehem and the preparations for the birth of Jesus. The second cantata opens quite differently and very atmospherically — who says Bach was not a romantic composer? — with the exquisite instrumental Pastoral Symphony, and goes on to describe the shepherds keeping their watch. The startling effect is slightly lost if the music is made to seem merely an interlude between one cantata and the next (which was what Handel did with his Pastoral Symphony, embedding it in the middle of Part One of *Messiah*). If a case is to be made for keeping Bach's cantatas separate, here is powerful evidence for it.

In the third cantata, we follow the shepherds to the manger and are told, in recitative, of their departure, 'glorifying and praising God for all the things that they had seen and heard'. The fourth cantata jumps to

New Year's Day, and tells of the circumcision and naming of the child. The fifth tells of the coming of the three wise men from the East, and ends with Herod's dismay at the news of Jesus' birth. The final cantata then returns to the subject of the three wise men, describing their gifts of gold, frankincense and myrrh. It ends optimistically with a chorale promising the salvation of mankind.

Each cantata, with the special exception of the second, opens with an extended chorus, leading to a recitative by the Evangelist; but thereafter the layout of the music changes with every cantata – in the third, for instance, the Evangelist's recitative leads to a further chorus, in the fourth to a subtle movement mingling recitative, arioso and chorale.

Though obviously related textually to Christmas, the *Christmas Oratorio* should not be regarded 'only' as a festive work – and to hear a performance at some other time is to be reminded of the fact. Much of the music comes from secular, non-Christmas cantatas which Bach had already written – like Handel, he was an expertly resourceful composer – and some of it, indeed, could be deemed more appropriate to its original secular text than to its Christmas one. Thus, in the famous aria 'Prepare thyself, Zion' in the first cantata, we may be struck by the serpentine bass part with which Bach underpins the music. Indeed, 'serpentine' is here the *mot juste*, for Bach originally wrote this aria for a cantata entitled *Hercules at the Crossroads*, in which the infant Hercules is attacked by snakes in his cradle.

Complete performances of the *Christmas Oratorio* can sometimes seem no more than acts of faith. In incompetent, old-fashioned hands, it can seem a very long work. But a good performance, with fine soloists, an alert chorus, bright-toned instrumentalists and a conductor expert in the art of Bachian pacing, is another matter. The days of stolid trudges through the *Christmas Oratorio* are a thing of the past, when a performance involved sitting for hours in a chilly church. Even when heard at home, on as many as four long-playing discs, it could seem to last an eternity.

Today's recordings need less space – just two CDs – and place the music in sharper perspective. Sharpest of all, as so often, is the combination of the Monteverdi Choir and English Baroque Soloists with John Eliot Gardiner as a conductor who permits no longueurs in his unfurling of the work's six episodes. The soloists, led by Anthony Rolfe Johnson's Evangelist, rise to the occasion, and the presence of Anne Sofie von Otter in music of such serene beauty speaks eloquently for itself (DG 423 232-2).

The suavely sensitive Masaaki Suzuki offers a very different experience with the support of Japan's Bach Collegium (BIS CD 941/2), but the finest *Christmas Oratorio* of them all is surely that of the Netherlands Bach Society, a performance so luminous and celebratory that the work springs to urgent new life. With his bright-toned choristers, period instrumentalists and peerless soloists, Jos van Veldhoven delivers the music with unfaltering verve. Accompanied by a lavish book of Nativity images from Utrecht's Catharine Convent and housed in a plush velvet box, this is a *Christmas Oratorio* gift-wrapped to the hilt — but don't be put off by the trappings. Here is a performance as truthful, eloquent and cheering as you will get (Channel Classics CCS SA 20103).

Sixteen

c.1735
Easter Oratorio, BWV 249

Sinfonia	Adagio	Chorus: Kommt, eilet und laufet
Recitative: O kalter Manner sinn		Aria: Seele, deine Spezereien
Recitative: Hier ist die Gruft		Aria: Sanfte soll mein Todeskummer
Recitative: Indessen seufzen wir		Aria: Saget, saget mir geschwinde
Recitative: Wir sind erfreut		Chorus: Preis und Dank

Bach was not Handel. He composed no operas, and had no desire to. Though there was drama in his life, he was never a man of the theatre. Egocentric, castrated opera singers and other such fripperies were things he could live without – he had quite enough trouble dealing with mean-minded church councils and pernickety royal courts. Of his three oratorios – which were not works on Handel's grandly theatrical lines – the most famous is really a set of six cantatas, one for each of the main feasts of Christmas. Performing the *Christmas Oratorio* as a Christmas oratorio was never Bach's intention.

The *Easter Oratorio*, on the other hand, comes somewhat closer to the Handelian meaning of the term. Conceived as an integer, it possesses dramatic continuity, even if Easter was not originally meant to be its subject. Its roots, in fact, were entirely secular, the music a birthday present for Duke Christian of Saxe-Weissenfels, the words paying tribute to his aristocratic virtues in a manner akin to that of a high-minded *opera seria*.

Yet, when the opportunity came to rewrite it, Bach was quick to respond. The nymphs and shepherds who had peopled the original text were transformed into Mary Magdalene, Mary the mother of James, and the disciples Peter and John. Then, having established their new identities, Bach in a further revision stripped them of their names. This, as Albert Schweitzer suggested, may have been because he considered the music insufficiently theatrical, but more probably it was because he took it for granted that his congregation would recognise without difficulty the unnamed characters – something which cannot be assumed of a twenty-first-century concert audience.

Theatrical it may not be, but dramatic it certainly is. The two opening movements, whatever their original intention, vividly survey the Easter story from different angles, first with joyous trumpets and drums, then in a tender *adagio* for oboe and strings. Mixed recitatives and arias deliver the action in a manner as operatic as Bach ever achieved. After the news of Christ's resurrection, there comes a rush to the tomb. At the centre of the work, a solo tenor sings an exquisite lullaby with rocking accompaniment for wind and soft violins.

Towards the end, trumpets and drums return, and the portals of heaven open. The tragedy of the *St Matthew Passion* is in the past. In its jubilation and brilliance, the *Easter Oratorio* is the obverse of that sombre work, as Paul McCreesh's fleet, sharp-edged recording of it with the Gabrieli Consort and Gabrieli Players makes exhilaratingly clear (Archiv 469 531-2).

The *Easter Oratorio*, however, was not Bach's only Easter journey. Producing 'well-regulated church music to the glory of God', which in Bach's case was synonymous with producing masterpieces, was a daily event in his life, certainly after he became cantor at St Thomas's, Leipzig, at the age of 38. Christmas, Easter and Whitsun were high points of the religious year, when something special was expected of him, and his ability to deliver what was necessary, even under pressure, was confirmed by two great – and greatly contrasted – Easter cantatas, Nos 6 and 66.

How Bach dealt with pressure was sometimes, as in the *Easter Oratorio*, a matter of pragmatism. So, too, with the Cantata No. 66, commemorating (in 1724) his first Easter in Leipzig. Though something new must have been expected of him, the work he supplied had in fact been written five years earlier as a birthday present for Prince Leopold of Anhalt-Cothen, whose musical interests were more secular than sacred, more instrumental than vocal. From that period dated many of Bach's concertos, sonatas and suites, as well as this cantata *Erfreut euch, ihr Herzen* ('Rejoice, ye hearts'), whose long opening chorus sounds more like the start of an enthusiastically celebratory ode than that of a serious church cantata. In his Leipzig recycling of the music, Bach changed the words but retained the high-speed exuberance.

The Cantata No. 6, *Bleib' bei uns* ('Abide with us'), on the other hand, is darker and more doleful. Composed for Easter the following year, it had been preceded on Good Friday by a revised version of the *St John Passion*, and its opening chorus sounds almost like a continuation of the sombre closing chorus of that work. The cantata expresses the sorrow of the disciples in music of haunting beauty, voiced by a solo contralto, tenor and bass, with a central chorale through which is threaded the eloquent strains of a violoncello piccolo.

Recordings of Bach's cantatas no longer possess rarity value; and John Eliot Gardiner's pilgrimage through all these works, begun on the 250th anniversary of the composer's death, is one of several such cycles. What separates this from the others, however, is that it is the outcome of a grand project whereby the works were to be performed on the correct feast days of the liturgical year in an array of atmospheric churches in Britain and elsewhere. Some of them were ones in which Bach himself had performed, though it was the remote Iona Abbey in Scotland – far beyond the composer's reach – which, on 28 July 2000, was reserved for the exact anniversary of his death.

Though Deutsche Grammophon pusillanimously backed out of the project after it had reached the tenth of a possible fifty discs, Gardiner and his performers – the indomitable Monteverdi Choir and English Baroque Soloists – bravely decided to forge ahead. To do so, he formed his own company named Soli Deo Gloria (based on the Latin tag with which Bach signed his scores, though the initials SDG suggest something ruder) in order to complete it, with Prince Charles as patron.

With performers so profoundly devoted to Bach, and so versed in his music, the pilgrimage proved more than a recording project. Some of the singing, not least Magdalena Kozena's in the solo cantata *Mein Herze schwimmt im Blut* ('My heart swims in blood') for the eleventh Sunday after Trinity, goes heart-rendingly beyond anything which Gardiner could originally have imagined. Intertwining with a solo oboe in the aria *Stumme Seufzer, stille Klagen* ('Wordless sighs, secret laments'), she makes Bach sound like Mahler.

As a chronicle of a year saturated in Bach's cantatas, the discs – thus far – rise to the occasion. The works themselves deserve nothing less. But the performances have an additional asset. Because Bach composed several complete (now, alas, in many instances incomplete) cantata cycles for the church year, Gardiner's decision to focus each performance on its feast day means that works written in different years are combined at times on a single disc.

In the case of the Cantatas Nos 6 and 66 – the one arrestingly the obverse of the other – this is invaluable. But, with Bernarda Fink, Michael Chance and Mark Padmore among the soloists, it is more than that. Every note is indelibly etched, both by these exquisite voices and by the instruments accompanying them. Listen to the combination of counter-tenor, tenor and solo violin in 'I used to fear the blackness of the grave', and you may wonder why Bach chose to compose no operas. But there is no point in wondering. This duet and its instrumental obbligato supply the answer (DG 463 580-2).

Seventeen

1742
GOLDBERG VARIATIONS, BWV 988

Whoever would have thought that Bach's *Goldberg Variations* for solo harpsichord – thirty private, studious, ruminative arabesques, written towards the middle of the eighteenth century for an audience of at most one person – would suddenly become a household hit, adored by performers and listeners around the world and now available in a bewildering variety of recordings?

Since Bach saw fit to publish the work soon after he wrote it, the vivid virtuosity, emotional range and sheer skill of the music could hardly fail to win a recognition wider than originally seemed likely. True, this took time. A performance attended by E. T. A. Hoffmann in 1810 prompted people to start walking out as early as Variation 4. Yet, partly through its built-in ability to refresh and enchant, partly through the intimacy of its sound-world, partly through its inexhaustibly sensuous sense of melody, it established a place in the Bach repertoire which became, and remains, entirely its own.

Fugue not being one of its priorities, it stands apart from *The Well-Tempered Clavier*, from *The Musical Offering* and above all from *The Art of Fugue* – works which in some respects it resembles. It exists purely for itself, successfully concealing its didacticism beneath its irresistible surface charm. That it is didactic, however, is not in doubt. Bach sternly and precisely described it as 'Keyboard Practice, consisting of an Aria with different variations for the harpsichord with two manuals', but added more congenially that it was 'prepared for the amusement of the souls of music-lovers' – a description of a sort he had already applied to his series of six keyboard partitas. These blurbs were his own, and he got their balance right. The intellectual side of the music added rigour to the romantic side. The romantic side added bloom to the rigour. Each aspect enhanced the other.

Viewed from one angle, the thirty variations are patterned with severe Bachian discipline in groups of three, each group consisting of a pair of dancelike or contrapuntal studies followed by a strict canon in which the right hand plays what the left hand has already played one bar earlier. Viewed from another angle, the effect is quite different. Instead of moving in threes, the movements seem to move in contrasted pairs, loud ones alternating with softer ones.

Either way, the ear is constantly misled by the fact that, as one astute commentator has observed, the canons tend to sound like variations and the variations like canons. What hardly any of them ever sounds like is the serene, sweet-toned, gravely dancing sarabande performed at the start, upon whose unhurried strains the entire work is based. These, it soon becomes apparent, are not variations in the Mozart manner, whereby a theme is exquisitely decorated but remains for the most part easily recognisable. What Bach, by a method familiar to jazz-lovers, here prefers to do is to employ the bass notes of the theme as the source of his inspiration rather than the theme itself. The result, far from being tuneless, is a cornucopian outpouring of melody.

For this reason, people today are perfectly content to sit back and let the music wash over them. Armed with the happy belief – or charming misconception – that Bach wrote the work for his pupil Johann Goldberg to play to Count Keyserlingk, the Russian ambassador to the Saxon Court at Dresden, as a cure for insomnia, they assume that what is being purveyed is some sort of gloriously extended lullaby. Though the intricate canons and variations which form the work's structure may seem at odds with this, such tokens of Bach's intellectual elitism fortunately do not interfere with anyone's enjoyment of the music.

Even if the tale of the sleepless listener were true – and the evidence remains flimsy – these thirty harpsichord pieces 'of a smooth and some-what lively nature' (as Bach's first biographer, Johann Forkel, called them) were never meant to be soporific. On the contrary, they could only have been designed to entertain him during his hours of chronic wakefulness. Today's listeners may know less than Keyserlingk about the difference between variations and canons, or between the two manuals of a harpsichord, but they are unlikely to find the music's vast melodious trajectory anything less than enthralling, or to fail to note that it incorporates some sudden and enlivening interruptions.

Of these, the most conspicuous derives from the way the work is assembled as a two-act music drama which, on reaching its exact midpoint, begins all over again. The signpost or turning point (to which some public performers draw extra attention by here unnecessarily inserting an interval) is Variation 16, which differs from the rest of the music by being an arresting French Ouverture in the form of a prelude and fugue, full of *majesté* and jerky French rhythms.

Three other variations draw attention to themselves by being written in dark G minor rather than the bright G major of their twenty-seven companions. Even listeners professing to have no sense of tonality will register these emotional plunges into the shadows of a key with which Mozart (Haydn also) would later become passionately associated. Their first occurrence is Variation 15, which brings part one of the work to its desolate close, in a manner reminiscent of what happens, more pictorially, in the middle of the early *Actus Tragicus* cantata.

The second occurrence, which casts a further cloud over the music, is the even more chromatic Variation 21, and the third is Variation 25, the longest, most brooding portion of the entire work, once likened by the great harpsichordist, Wanda Landowska, to a 'black pearl'. In this extended keyboard fantasy, with its romantic harmonies and yearning oboe-like melodic line, Bach reaches forward to the nocturnal music of Chopin in the same way as Chopin, in some of his slow nocturnes and other pieces, seems to be meditating on Bach.

The ascents from these depths prove as startling as the plunges into them, the sense of release ultimately provided by Variation 26 being exhilaratingly palpable. Shimmering sprays of notes sustain the momentum from here right through to the humour of the closing *quodlibet* (meaning a medley, or 'what you please'), whereby two jocular German pop songs of the period merge in an uninhibitedly festive farewell. Some performances end unsentimentally at this point. Others, with the composer's blessing, recapitulate the slow opening sarabande whose simplicity of utterance is tenderly regained, in spite of all the technical and emotional baggage which has been picked up en route.

Today, performances of the *Goldberg Variations* are given in large halls or small, in churches or barns, on harpsichords or pianos, by performers who play them straightforwardly or intricately, too fast, too slow, or, in a minority of cases, at what seems the perfect tempo. The first of two recordings by Glenn Gould, the mercurial Canadian pianist, was one of the quickest, lasting only half as long as the last recording by Rosalyn Tureck, a pianist famed for her slow speeds, none of them less hurried or more illuminating than in this final product of her extreme old age.

Never was Bach's music distilled to such perfection as by Tureck. The clock, however, is no judge of the *Goldberg Variations*. Neither, for that matter, is choice of instrument. The employment of a piano does not conflict with Bach's specification of a two-manual harpsichord, except quite literally in certain passages where the pianist's hands, with only one keyboard at their disposal, happen to collide.

Yet, to insist that only a harpsichord can supply the timbres Bach intended is to cut yourself off from Gould, Tureck, Perahia, Schiff and other pianists with deep understanding of the music. Bach himself, alert to the possibilities of the early Silbermann piano, manufactured by one of his friends, was no opponent of the art of transcription. The *Goldberg Variations*, through their emotional range, have become a pinnacle of the pianist's art, just as they are a pinnacle of the harpsichordist's.

Assessing a performance by the stopwatch, however, is just as restrictive. Nuances of rhythm and tempo can make a fast performance sound slow and a slow performance sound fast. But, in this work, there is in any case another factor, whose effect on the music is profound. Since each variation, like the theme itself, falls into two parts, and since each part is marked with a repeat sign, performers must decide from the start whether they are going to follow what may seem to some people to be the composer's tiresomely methodical and repetitive instructions.

Impatient players tend to repeat the first part but not the second, with the result that, in terms of structure, each variation is lopsidedly balanced. Others, even less patient (like Gould in his first recording), observe no repeats at all, which results in better balance but can seem like a ride straight down a motorway. Some include the repeats in the short fast variations but omit them in the long slow ones, a process which, for all its practicality, seems like portion control, resulting in a performance in which all the variations are roughly the same length. This is not a good idea.

Choosing a recording therefore depends on your own as well as the performer's priorities. Tureck gives us every note; and the music, while demanding patience of the listener, surely benefits. Gustav Leonhardt favours slow speeds and exquisite harpsichord timbres, but his performance, through his shunning of repeats, is one of the shortest. Pierre Hantai supremely justifies the sonorities of a harpsichord, but both his recordings are marred by touches of aggressiveness. Schiff and Perahia are pianists who give us the repeats, along with their own fascinating programme notes; but Schiff's quirky shaping of the main theme yields to Perahia's more natural one.

Which to choose? Put your money on Tureck, for her sheer beauty of tone, articulation of ornaments, thoughtfulness and calm determination to make the music set its own unhurried pace. Though her performance requires two discs, it is entirely worth this extravagance (DG 459599-2).

Eighteen

1747
THE MUSICAL OFFERING, BWV 1079

Bach composed *The Musical Offering*, followed by *The Art of Fugue*, in what was literally the twilight of his life, when cataracts were clouding his vision and he had the misfortune to come under the knife of the touring English eye surgeon, John Taylor, who operated on Handel eight years later with similarly disastrous results. To claim that Bach's ensuing blindness and death were entirely Taylor's 'fault' would doubtless be to exaggerate. Such things can happen even today, at a time when cataract surgery – which the author of this book has successfully undergone on both his eyes – has become a predominantly safe, speedy, painless, untraumatic procedure.

There is no doubt, however, that Taylor was over-optimistic when he reported that his treatment of the 'celebrated master of music' in Leipzig in 1750 went well. Carl Philipp Emanuel, writing his delayed obituary of his father four years later, reported that not only did the operation require to be repeated but also 'it went very badly'. Bach's general health deteriorated quickly. His musical duties became a burden. The Leipzig authorities, anticipating his death, insensitively began looking for a successor. Meanwhile, the composer was retreating deeper and deeper into himself, concentrating his mind on what seemed to be the pure mathematical counterpoint of his last works.

But what counterpoint! And what resourcefulness! Inspired by his last long journey – to visit the nerve-racked Carl Philipp Emanuel at Frederick the Great's court in Potsdam – *The Musical Offering* owes its existence to the king's reaction to Bach's arrival at the newly built Palace of Sans-Souci. 'Ladies and gentlemen', Frederick reputedly declared, 'old Bach is here.'

The reference to Bach's age may or may not have been derogatory – Frederick's taste was for the fierier, edgier music of young Carl Philipp Emanuel. But, for the first and only time in his life, Bach found himself featured on the front page of a Berlin newspaper, though the vain Prussian king was inevitably given pride of place in the report of what happened when the two men met. Tradition has it that the composer-king condescended to play a theme of his own on his new fortepiano and asked the short-sighted Bach to improvise a fugue on it.

In doing so – as the newspaper reported – 'Mr Bach found the subject propounded to him so beautiful that he intends to set it down on paper'. Thus was *The Musical Offering* first offered to King Frederick, and the fortepiano which formed its starting point can still be viewed in the king's music room along with the flute upon which the belligerent king was a famed exponent. But the subject, whether or not Frederick actually wrote it, was certainly beautiful and, it must be said, utterly Bachian in its progress from minor-key simplicity to poignant, haunting chromaticism. Out of it, Bach appeared to have had no trouble drawing the fugues, canons and inspired four-movement trio sonata which form the vast remainder of the work.

Sometimes performed complete but more often in excerpt form, *The Musical Offering* is a magnificent cornucopia of counterpoint, every moment of which reveals some special facet of Bach's genius. As with the subsequent *The Art of Fugue*, he was by no means specific about which instruments he had in mind for its performance; but it would seem that some portions were intended for keyboard, some for a combination of King Frederick's flute, violin and continuo, and some for a chamber ensemble of one sort or another. A variety of arrangements of it exist, one of them by the conductor Claudio Abbado, directed by him at the 1967 Edinburgh Festival in the spacious surroundings of the Usher Hall.

For Bach, it was the music that mattered, not the instruments chosen to perform it. The theme itself is heard at its most eloquent in the so-called *Ricercare* – in essence a sort of free fugue in six parts, gradually intensifying as it proceeds, and fascinating enough to prompt the vanguard twentieth-century composer Anton Webern to produce his own inspired arrangement of it for chamber ensemble. But the way in which the royal theme slides in and out of the Trio Sonata is no less compelling, its chromatic contours always instantly recognisable, no matter whether they appear at the top of the texture or the bottom. There is pathos here, and passion. But it is the sheer versatility of which the ailing Bach here proved capable that is constantly astounding, sustained right through to the end of the vivaciously jigging finale.

Complete recordings of *The Musical Offering* are in strangely short supply. Though the music will never have the mass appeal of the Brandenburg concertos, it does not deserve to be written off as a prolonged demonstration of elitist, scholarly note-spinning. Yet its very richness can seem self-defeating. Did Bach intend its thirteen portions to be performed as an entity, like the *Goldberg Variations*, or simply as a contrapuntal reservoir to be dipped into? Much, surely, depends on the quality of the performance. A poor one – and too many of them are poor – merely meanders. A good one steadily intensifies.

Coupled with *The Art of Fugue*, the recording of *The Musical Offering* by Reinhard Goebel's Musica Antiqua Köln may sound like contrapuntal overkill. But the performances, which include an encore in the form of the fourteen recently discovered canons which Bach wrote on a page of his own copy of the *Goldberg Variations*, combine scholarly know-how with instrumental verve (Archiv 413 642-2). Though there are separate recordings of *The Musical Offering*, no other wholly matches the atmosphere of this.

Nineteen

1749
MASS IN B MINOR, BWV 232

Kyrie   Gloria   Credo   Sanctus   Agnus Dei

Bach's output, vast in bulk, contains every kind of music which was fashionable in his lifetime, except opera. His stern Lutheran outlook, it would be easy to surmise, distanced him from the world of the theatre in a way that made him a quite different sort of composer from his more flamboyantly sophisticated London-based contemporary, George Frideric Handel, whose oratorios, though written to glorify God, were entertainment music in exactly the same sense as his operas. Bach's attitude to opera was encapsulated in his sarcastic remark to one of his sons: 'Well, Friedemann, shall we go to Dresden and hear the pretty tunes?'

Yet to describe Bach's B minor Mass purely as church music would be as misleading as to call Michelangelo's *Last Judgement* simply a church decoration. Whatever Bach's original intentions for it actually were – and even today they seem not wholly clear – it undoubtedly breaks their bounds. Unlike his cantatas, it is too big to form a musical interlude in a church service. Unlike the *St Matthew Passion*, it does not tell a story. As an entity, it remained unperformed, largely unknown, and unpublished until 1818, nearly seventy years after its provincial German composer's death.

Thereafter, however, it gradually became a world treasure, part of the well-spring of Western music, perhaps the greatest of innumerable masterpieces poured forth by Bach in the way of business, a work whose title 'Mass in B minor' automatically identifies its composer. Today it is performed by forces large or small, in surroundings grand or intimate. To present it in a theatre hardly constitutes sacrilege. The music, as its resounding opening notes assert, is high drama from the hand of a composer with an instinctive sense of what was dramatic. Its colouring, like its style, is infinitely richer than might be expected of someone famed for Protestant austerity. Every facet of it is a separate art in itself.

In spite of the piecemeal (not to say desultory) way in which it was written, it is also an integer – perhaps the most extraordinary of its kind. Its beginnings were modest and functional. In the summer of 1733, the Protestant Bach delivered a Latin Kyrie and Gloria – the two portions of a Mass common to both Lutheran and Roman services – to the newly crowned Augustus III, Elector of Saxony and King of Poland, as evidence of his qualifications for the post of Court Music Director. With the music went a promise to 'show indefatigable industry in the composition of church music'. Since he was already the cantor, or music director, of Leipzig's main church, and had already written plenty of polonaises as well as the *St Matthew Passion*, his credentials were good. But the king, who had more important matters on his mind, took three years to tell him that the job was his.

Not until twelve years later did Bach complete the enormous edifice we now know as the B minor Mass, working on it mostly in his spare time. He had no specific reason to do so, other perhaps than a growing awareness of his own mortality – he died soon after writing it. Like *The Art of Fugue*, indeed, it appears to have been composed primarily for his own satisfaction. As was his custom, he recycled some of the music from earlier works, though most of the arias – which are among the glories of the finished product – were new.

To speak of Bach's 'so-called' Mass in B minor, as some authorities still do, is therefore misleading. In spite of its complex and protracted history, the work possesses an identifiable ground-plan, not least in its choice of keys. Not for nothing does the sound of D major (the obverse of B minor) permeate the music at crucial moments; not for nothing is its presence sensationally highlighted by the use of trumpets and kettledrums at these points; not for nothing does a work that begins in sombre B minor starkness end in D major radiance.

Between the buttresses of its opening and closing movements, the B minor Mass has an internal structure that seems by no means haphazard. Grand choruses are followed by lyrical arias. Fast choruses are counterbalanced by majestic or plaintive choruses. The choice of obbligato instruments in the arias not only seems scrupulously, indeed mathematically, pre-planned, but also forms an overall distinctive pattern. Yet Bach also knew the value of unpredictability. One of the most curious obbligato sonorities – a combination of horn and two bassoons – is exploited only once, to maximum effect. Bach's keen ear for timbre, indeed, is never more marked than in portions of this work, and nothing is more perfectly textured than the *Domine Deus* section of the Gloria, where the solo soprano and tenor sing what has been described as a 'devotional love duet' – a pretty tune, whether Bach would have called it that or not – against an exquisitely poised background of solo flute, muted violins and violas, pizzicato cello and bass.

Yet, for all its delicacy of utterance, there was a time when the B minor Mass was regarded, in Britain at least, solely as a vehicle for large-scale, slow-moving forces. Albert Coates, in conducting it, used to demand that the organist draw the thirty-two-foot pedal reed for the striding bass octaves in the Sanctus. Edinburgh's Sir Donald Tovey, in a vivid phrase, claimed that the strings in this movement represented the swinging of censers. When conducted by Otto Klemperer, the five-part fugue that forms the opening Kyrie could sound like the inexorable grinding of some enormous piece of liturgical machinery.

Today, on the other hand, the use of very small forces, and parity of numbers between voices and instruments, have proved that clarity of texture, sharpness of outline, freshness and variety of colour can all be achieved without loss of drama. But, whichever way it is presented, the B minor Mass remains a musical cornucopia. The wide range of available recordings stresses this point.

You can have it conducted big-scale by Herbert von Karajan, Carlo Maria Giulini and Eugen Jochum (who asserted that 'authentic' Bach was strictly for vegetarians). These performances, though they tend to sound lumbering, often have the advantage of star soloists – Dame Janet Baker in the Giulini set, Elisabeth Schwarzkopf in the Karajan – unmatchable today.

Compared with the intimacy of Konrad Junghanel's recording with the Cantus Cölln, however, they seem to belong to a different era. Junghanel employs no world-renowned soloists. The solo parts are sung by members of his small choir, just as Bach himself would have expected. As a result, the performance is wholly unified. The gentle halo of sound, penetrated where necessary by bright trumpet tone, is proof that Bach, even in his grandest works, was a purveyor of musical magic (Harmonia Mundi HMC 801813-14).

Twenty

1750
THE ART OF FUGUE, BWV 1080

To listen to all ninety-odd minutes of *The Art of Fugue* in a single sitting used to be considered the most daunting musical experience of them all, surpassed (for those who managed to hear a performance of it) only by the four hours of Sorabji's *Opus Clavicembalisticum*. At the end, once Bach's fourteen fugues and four canons had run their unhurried contrapuntal course, you could understand why Hubert Parry, the Victorian composer and scholar, declared that the music was never actually intended for performance.

It was Bach's final achievement, a grand summing-up of his lifelong mastery of counterpoint, a detailed reminder that music in those days was a branch of mathematics. His rapidly failing health and his by then almost total blindness prevented him from finishing it — or so it was said. Whether, as is now believed, the clinching pages were accidentally lost, or never got written down, the music could not end more suddenly and dramatically than it does, in the course of a final quadruple fugue based partly on the letters of Bach's name in German notation. In a good performance, the way in which the music suddenly stops in its tracks carries impressive shock value. But, because Bach left the work in open score – that is, without specifying which instruments were meant to play it – nobody has ever known what his intentions for his last masterpiece actually were.

Sir Donald Tovey, Edinburgh University's essayist and professor of music, convinced himself that it was written for a single keyboard, even though the music was spread over four staves – like a string quartet – rather than the two or three conventionally required by a harpsichord or organ. To show how Bach himself might have ended it, Tovey proceeded to complete the awe-inspiring final quadruple fugue himself, and then record it on the piano.

Other authorities, finding the sound of a solo instrument too restrictive for music such as this, have preferred to think of *The Art of Fugue* in terms of ensemble music. As a result, various versions of it now exist, offering a choice of instrumentations: for two pianos, two harpsichords, string quartet, wind quintet, string sextet, string orchestra, mixed strings and woodwind, a line-up of brass, a consort of viols, an electronic synthesiser.

Ingenuity of this sort, however, tends not to simplify the music but to complicate it further. The secret of *The Art of Fugue*, like that of all Bach, lies in its beauty of line, which is why it works so well on the keyboard. In this respect, only the string quartet provides a viable (some would say superior) alternative through its ability to identify all the strands of Bach's texture and turn the four fugal voices into a music drama for four combined yet distinctive personalities. True, if the feat is to be achieved, the viola requires to be enlarged to unplayable dimensions or at the very least provided with some sort of extended bottom register – a factor fascinatingly explored by the Indian writer, Vikram Seth, in his beautiful and knowledgeable novel about the members of a string quartet, *An Equal Music*.

Bach, as we have now realised, did not compose *The Art of Fugue* in a single surge of inspiration. He worked on it, off and on, for many years, while his health was gradually failing. Yet the entire score sounds thoroughly unified by the opening theme, which serves as the fountainhead of all the movements that follow. What seems to have delayed the final perfecting of the music was the question of the running order of the fugues, on each of which Bach somewhat severely bestowed the Latin title 'Contrapunctus'. As a result, performers have felt entitled to make changes of their own, and sometimes to omit movements, in a way nobody would dream of doing in the case of the *Goldberg Variations*.

But then, *The Art of Fugue* is a very different sort of work, more pared down in its material, more controlled, abstract, slow-moving, more focused on its dark-toned home key of D minor, more relentlessly *fugal* –

and considerably longer. The inspirational opening theme is not – as that of the *Goldbergs* certainly is – a haunting, dreamy, exquisitely nocturnal dance, but something infinitely starker, more angular, more recognisably a foreground or background presence as the work goes through its unhurried motions. No matter what Bach does with it, it – or something like it – seldom moves wholly out of earshot, whereas in the *Goldbergs* the return of the theme at the end always comes as a romantic surprise, the most perfect of all postludes.

Though *The Art of Fugue* could never be called romantic in that sense, it is nevertheless a strangely moving and enthralling work, once you begin to know it. Just as mathematicians have been said to weep at the beauty of numbers, so the very austerity of *The Art of Fugue* embodies its own emotional charge. Each contrapuntal variation on the theme – whose inspired simplicity, even on paper, speaks for itself – becomes mysteriously more expressive than the one before. This is not something that happens in the ever-changing forty-eight preludes and fugues, which are a different experience altogether; but it is present in the repetitions of *A Musical Offering* before Bach's obsessiveness achieved its final perfection in *The Art of Fugue*.

Getting to know *The Art of Fugue*, however, requires time and patience. For the listener, it is not musical wallpaper. From the performer, it requires supreme authority. As Alfred Brendel once perceptively remarked, it is not music to be meddled with. Nor is it heard to advantage in a concert hall, unless the performance and its surroundings are absolutely right. For this reason, perhaps the best approach route to what can seem a stern and impassable *massif* is via a recording by a trusted exponent.

Of the discs available, at least two possess the combination of wisdom and imagination which the music demands. For a statement of the work in all its keyboard purity, Davitt Moroney's performance on a clear, silver-toned harpsichord is all that could be desired in terms of beauty, intensity and modern scholarship (Harmonia Mundi HMA 1951169-70). The valuable liner notes are by the performer himself, who is also the author of a short but valuable book on Bach.

If, in comparison, the Emerson Quartet's case for presenting *The Art of Fugue* as a masterpiece for strings – poised somewhere between a layman's guide to mathematical philosophy and Beethoven's late quartets – seems something of a soft sell, it is nevertheless fascinating enough to be well worth acquiring. Coming from these famously high-powered players, this is undoubtedly a performance with a capital 'P'. It has passion, speed, terseness, fullness of tone, a viola which sounds as broad as a house, fierce intensity of expression and a dramatic awareness of the effect of leaving the last note hanging in the air. What it does not have is a sense of period style. In such a context, however, this could seem irrelevant (DG 474 495-2).

For keen variety of colour, without loss of period style, Reinhard Goebel and Musica Antiqua Köln, playing on baroque instruments, offer a masterly and irreproachable survey of the music (Archiv 447 293-2).

FURTHER READING

Malcolm Boyd, *Bach* (Dent, 1983; Oxford, 2000)

Useful and thorough life-and-works in the long-established *Master Musicians* series.

Karl Geiringer, *Johann Sebastian Bach: The Culmination of an Era* (Allen & Unwin, 1966; Oxford, 1966)

A milestone in the history of Bach biography. Though inevitably dated, it remains worth reading, not least for its scholarly perception and warmheartedness.

Davitt Moroney, *Bach: An Extraordinary Life* (Associated Board of the Royal Schools of Music, 2000)

Though aimed at a student readership, this is a lively and concentrated modern study which assembles its information lucidly and never gets bogged down in inessentials.

Alec Robertson, *The Church Cantatas of J. S. Bach* (Cassell, 1972; Praeger Publishers, 1972)

Encyclopaedic survey of the 200-or-so surviving works. Not new, but an indispensable bible of the music for those who have embarked – or plan to embark – on a personal odyssey through its riches.

Peter Williams, *Bach: The Goldberg Variations* (Cambridge, 2001)

Detailed, blow-by-blow study of one of the peaks of Bach's output. Best read before, during and after a performance – or CD – of the work. The introduction, which occupies half the book, sets the scene. Academic, but beautifully and vividly written by an authority who is himself a gifted exponent of the music.

Peter Williams, *The Life of Bach* (Cambridge, 2004)

Excellent, precise, thoroughly up-to-date biography by a leading English Bach scholar who does not fail to mention the works and who has chilling things to say of the Leipzig background against which the *St Matthew Passion* was composed.

Christoph Wolff, *Johann Sebastian Bach: The Learned Musician* (Oxford, 2001)

Substantial, important millennial study, strong on church music, less stern than its title suggests, but over-devoted to lists.

GLOSSARY

Adagio. Italian term for 'slow', often interpreted as very slow. But can also mean 'comfortable'.

Allegro. Italian term for 'light' or 'fast'. But is an 'allegretto' (meaning, literally, 'a little allegro') slower or faster than allegro? The term is usually accepted as meaning slower, but is irritatingly ambiguous.

Andante. Italian term for 'at walking pace'.

Aria. Italian term for 'air' or 'song'.

Arioso. A recitative with the lyrical quality of an aria.

Arpeggio. Split chord, i.e. a chord whose notes are spread in a harplike manner instead of being sounded simultaneously.

Baritone. Singer whose voice range lies between that of a tenor and a bass.

Cadenza. Solo passage of varying length, particularly in the first movement of a concerto or in a vocal work, enabling the soloist to display his/her technique in an improvisational manner relevant to the work being performed. Brandenburg Concerto No. 5 contains an inspired harpsichord cadenza.

Canon. Passage in which a melody performed by one instrument or voice is taken up by another before the previous voice has finished.

Cantata. A vocal work, often but not necessarily of a religious nature, usually involving solo voices and chorus with orchestra.

Chamber orchestra. Smallish orchestra, usually of up to about forty players, suitable for performing in surroundings more intimate than a large concert hall. Though chamber orchestras have their own established repertoire, symphony orchestras frequently intrude on it, just as chamber orchestras today increasingly invade the symphony orchestra's territory, often with conspicuous, indeed revelatory, success.

Chromatic. Put simply, a scale which moves in semitones or, in piano terms, one which uses all the black notes as well as the white notes of the keyboard. Chromatic harmony is thus richer than diatonic harmony, which involves only the notes of the normal major or minor scales.

Coda. Italian term for 'tail' or 'tailpiece'. The closing section of a movement.

Concerto. A work for solo instrument (or instruments) and orchestra, involving responses between one and the other.

Counterpoint. The combination of two or more melodies or musical figures in such a way that they make musical sense.

Fantasy. A mood piece of some sort, free-ranging and (at least seemingly) improvisational in style. In Bach's day, a fantasy tended to be an elaborate and contrapuntal keyboard piece, often for organ.

Finale. The concluding movement of a work (e.g. symphony, string quartet, sonata) in several movements.

Fugue. A type of composition, movement, or section of a movement involving a given number of instruments or voices which enter separately, at different pitches, in imitation of each other.

Gavotte. Old French dance in duple time.

Larghetto. Italian term for 'slow and dignified'.

Largo ma non tanto. Italian term meaning 'slowly but not too slowly'.

Menuett. German term for 'minuet'. A courtly dance in 3/4 time.

Minuet. Dance in triple-time, usually employed by Bach as a movement towards the end of a suite for solo instrument (violin, cello or harpsichord) or orchestra. The contrasted middle section of a minuet is known as a trio, because there was a tradition for writing it in three-part harmony, though Bach also used the term 'Minuet Two'.

Moderato. Italian term for 'at moderate speed'.

Opera. Music drama or 'sung play', in which the cast sing their roles rather than speak them – though speech is employed in some operas, including, most expressively, Beethoven's *Fidelio*. A vital component of opera is the orchestra, providing far more than a mere accompaniment, with a chorus, large or small, supplying another (though not essential) dramatic dimension. Opera as we know it was born in Italy around 1600, spreading to France, Germany, Austria and other countries, and inspiring many cities to build their own opera houses for its performance. The places where Bach lived tended not to possess opera houses, which may help to explain his contempt for opera – though who knows whether he would have been tempted to write such works if there had been an opera house handy?

Ouverture. French word for 'overture', frequently employed by Bach. The word can also mean 'suite', Bach's four orchestral suites being thus named.

Pizzicato. Plucked note on a string instrument.

Presto. Italian term for very fast.

Rondo form. Italian term for what was traditionally the spirited finale of a symphony, string quartet or sonata. The word refers to the fact that the opening theme or section of the movement keeps recurring, or coming 'round' again, thereby forming an essential part of the music's structure. Slow movements can also be in rondo form. Bach's *Christmas Oratorio* has been described as a huge rondo.

Scherzo. Italian term for 'joke'. Title applied by Beethoven, and to a lesser extent by Haydn, to what until then had been a movement in the form of a minuet. Scherzos came after Bach's time, though some movements by him show scherzo-like tendencies.

Sonata. A work for one or two instruments, usually consisting of three or four carefully structured and contrasted movements.

Soprano. The highest female voice, ranging from middle C upwards.

Sostenuto. Italian term for 'sustained'.

Staccato. Italian term for 'short and detached'. Opposite of *legato*, meaning smooth. Signified by a dot over the printed note.

Symphony. Form of orchestral work in several movements, usually of an ambitious nature. Much favoured by Haydn (known as the 'father of the symphony'), Mozart, Beethoven, Schubert, Mendelssohn, Brahms and their successors. Bach employed the Italian word 'sinfonia', which at that time was synonymous with overture.

Tenor. High male voice, employed for narrative effect by Bach in his St Matthew and St John Passions.

Tonic. The keynote of a scale. For example, the keynote of the scale of C is the note C.

Tranquillo. Italian term for 'tranquil'.

Tremolo. Italian term for 'trembling'. The rapid 'trembling' repetition of a single note, or alternation between two notes.

Trill. Musical term for the rapid alternation of the written note and the note above. Trills are traditionally decorative, but in keyboard terms they are a way of sustaining the sound of a note.

Trio. A word with several musical meanings: (1) a work for three instruments, (2) the ensemble which performs such a work, and

(3) the name of the middle section of a minuet or scherzo, so called because at one time it was written in three-part harmony. A 'trio sonata' in Bach's day confusingly required four instruments.

Triplet. A group of three notes of equal duration, written where some other quantity of notes (perhaps just a single note) is implied by the time signature.

Vibrato. Italian term for the rapid vibration in pitch produced by instrumentalists or singers in their performance of a piece of music. Exaggerated vibrato is often described, disparagingly, as 'wobble'. As the history of the symphony orchestra progressed during the twentieth century, so the use of vibrato increased. But in Bach's day, performances were vibrato-less, and today many specialist players and orchestras have been learning, with greater and greater success, how to recreate the original sound. Though some listeners regret the loss of a warm bath of vibrato-laden string tone, the compensations in terms of incisiveness and authenticity are manifest.

Vivace. Italian term for 'lively'.